29.95

G000068271

# The Widowed Self

## The Older Woman's Journey through Widowhood

Deborah Kestin van den Hoonaard

**Wilfrid Laurier University Press**

[WLU]

This book has been published with the help of a grant from the Humanities and Social Sciences Federation of Canada, using funds provided by the Social Sciences and Humanities Research Council of Canada. We acknowledge the support of the Canada Council for the Arts for our publishing program. We acknowledge the financial support of the Government of Canada through the Book Publishing Industry Development Program for our publishing activities.

### Canadian Cataloguing in Publication Data

Van den Hoonaard, Deborah K. (Deborah Kestin), 1951-
  The widowed self : the older woman's journey through widowhood

Includes bibliographical references and index.
ISBN 0-88920-346-6

1. Widowhood. 2. Widows — New Brunswick. I. Title.

HQ1058.V36 2001           306.88           C99-932479-9

© 2001 Wilfrid Laurier University Press
Waterloo, Ontario  N2L 3C5

Cover design by Leslie Macredie,
using a pastel by Suzanne Maloney entitled *Énigme*

Printed in Canada

All rights reserved. No part of this work covered by the copyrights hereon may be reproduced or used in any form or by any means—graphic, electronic or mechanical—without the prior written permission of the publisher. Any request for photocopying, recording, taping or reproducing in information storage and retrieval systems of any part of this book shall be directed in writing to the Canadian Reprography Collective, 214 King Street West, Suite 312, Toronto, Ontario  M5H 3S6.

*This book is dedicated with love to my sister, Ricki Kestin, who always challenged me to be more than I thought I could be.*

*And to my parents, Krass and Estelle Kestin, whose love and confidence in me have seen me through all the days of my life.*

# Contents

# Acknowledgements

*I*'ve always felt that writing acknowledgements must be the most entertaining part of writing a book and the most humbling. You get to sit around and try to remember everybody who had a part in your writing your book—and, as has been said many times before—writing a book is never an individual achievement.

First, thanks must go to the women who shared their stories of losing their husbands and attempting to rebuild their lives. This was often a painful experience for them, but they shared many confidences with me and have inspired me with their courage and resilience. Many mentioned that they hope their participation in the study will help others.

Helena Z. Lopata carried out the first major study on widowhood, and she has encouraged my interest in the topic. All who study widowhood have benefited from her groundbreaking work, and, on a more personal level, she has always prodded me to work at a higher level.

Others at Loyola University of Chicago, where I completed my Ph.D., have been instrumental in encouraging my interest in widowhood. Christine L. Fry, co-director of my dissertation with Helena Lopata, and Judith Wittner both have maintained an interest in my work and have contributed to my ability to do good qualitative work.

Howard S. Becker allowed me to sit in on his Field Methods course at Northwestern University and was a member of my dissertation committee as well. The stories of his experiences in research are a true inspiration. I also appreciate being able to keep up with his work by simply clicking on to "Howie's Home Page" on the Internet.

The Third Age Centre at St. Thomas University in Fredericton, New Brunswick, was a partner in the research. Its then-director, Mary Lou Arseneault, first encouraged me to apply for research funding. Her enthusiasm for the project has been unflagging, and the friendship that has resulted is precious. Others at the Third Age Centre, notably Chris Korth and Kerry Smith, provided excellent administrative support. Shelley Coyle prepared the more than 2,000 pages of interview transcripts. Mary Radford and Rachel Matchett helped to develop the six-week "Striving on Your Own" workshop that the Third Age Centre put on when my plans to observe a local support group fell through. Ann Ingram of *The Daily Gleaner* wrote a number of articles about the research.

Although a book is written in solitude, the enthusiasm and encouragement of others can keep you going when you feel that the manuscript will never be finished. Colleagues at St. Thomas University showed unwavering interest in my work. I would particularly like to mention John McKendy, Sandra Wachholz, Gary Kenyon, Bill Randall and Penny Granter. As well, participants at the Annual Qualitative Analysis Conference put up with and were even excited about papers based on this project for several years in a row. Karen March has been particularly supportive. Other friends, particularly Tim and Bev Rayne, had a continuing interest in the book which never ceased to motivate me to finish.

The research on which this book is based was funded by a Community Researcher Award of the Seniors' Independence Research Program of Health Canada (NHRDP award no. 6604-111-603). A pilot project was funded by the Grants to Small Universities Program of the Social Sciences and Humanities Research Council of Canada.

Sandra Woolfrey, formerly of WLU Press, was unfailingly helpful, and she helped shepherd me through the Aid to Scholarly Publications Program process. Others at the Press, notably Carroll Klein and Leslie Macredie, have been most helpful in the later stages of preparation.

Families of authors always seem to occupy the final paragraph of acknowledgements. My three children, Lisa-Jo, Lynn (aka Cheryl) and Jordan always made me feel that my writing this book is important to them—and they have listened to hundreds of hours of my talk about the project at meals. My husband, Will, makes such a profound contribution to everything I do that there are no words to describe it. From keeping a chart of my progress on his filing cabinet to telling everyone he meets about my work, his actions display a profound belief in both the importance of this book and my ability to write it that is almost overwhelming.

# Introduction

*T*his book is about how older women experience widowhood. I first became interested in this topic when a student lent me a book called *When Things Get Back to Normal* (Dohaney 1989), a published journal of the author's first year of widowhood. It took me two hours to read the book, and I found myself crying along with the author and feeling that, for the first time, I was at the beginning of understanding the profound impact that losing one's husband has on one's life. This was a far cry from the dry literature on "social support" and "well-being" that I had encountered in most of my reading in the area of gerontology in general, and widowhood in particular.[1]

*When Things Get Back to Normal* had such an impact on me that I found myself seeking out any published, autobiographical accounts of widowhood that I could find. These accounts were universally moving and evocative, and they convinced me that hearing widows' stories in their own words would shed a much more comprehensive light on the social meaning of widowhood as well as allow us to catch a glimpse of the profound emotional ordeal that is at the core of that experience.

The women who wrote these accounts underwent a pivotal loss of identity, "identity foreclosure" (van den Hoonaard 1997), through which they felt stripped of who they were at every level—they did not know how to define themselves to themselves, and they became different people to

Notes to the Introduction are on p. 12.

1

their friends, who in large number excluded them from their previous social groups. These authors report that this crisis of identity led to the development of a new and, according to the authors, a more mature identity.

But the authors of published accounts were young-to-middle-aged women who had the personal resources that resulted in the publishing of books. What of older women? Would they experience the same loss of sense of who they are? How would they go about rebuilding their lives after losing someone to whom they had been married for thirty, forty or fifty years? How do older women experience and talk about being widows?

To answer these questions I chose a research process that would allow me to look at women's experience of widowhood as a process of transition rather than simply as a status. In-depth, narrative interviews provide an opportunity for people to tell their own story in their own way, including whatever they feel is necessary. As Daniel Bertaux (1981, 39) has pointed out, "A good life story is one in which the interviewee *takes over control of the interview situation* and talks freely" (emphasis in original).

I conducted interviews between August 1994 and January 1996 with twenty-seven women in a variety of urban and rural locales throughout New Brunswick.[2] The interviews took place in each woman's home and lasted between two and four hours. The design of the interview schedule was very open and sparse, allowing the women who participated in the study to frame their own stories in their own ways, and to include or leave out whatever they chose. I had an idea of what themes I wanted to cover in the interviews, but the widows certainly brought in issues I had not anticipated and demonstrated that they define their experience as widows in a way that reflects continuity within their own lives.

To provide an opportunity and encourage each woman to bring in any issues she thought relevant, I first asked her to recount her experience as a widow:

> What I would like for you to do now is just tell me about your experience
> with being a widow. You can start where you want, end where you want, put
> in whatever you like, leave out whatever you like. I'm just interested in find-
> ing out about your experience.[3]

The intention of this request was to allow each woman to recount the social meaning of widowhood from her point of view, an intrinsic characteristic of research carried out from a symbolic interactionist perspective. This book reflects this approach, and explores older women's experiences of widowhood in a way that has not been reflected in most studies on the subject.

The next few pages of this introduction will explain how the research on which this book is based differs from more traditional ways of studying widowhood, as well as the assumptions of symbolic interactionism and the impact they have on the manner of presentation of empirical data and theoretical insights in this book.

The first major study on widowhood was published over twenty-five years ago (Lopata 1973). Helena Lopata's books *Widowhood in an American City* (1973) and *Women as Widows* (1979) still stand as virtually the only books that provide a comprehensive exploration of widowhood. Since that time there have been many studies focused on smaller aspects of widowhood, and three themes have dominated this research: the psychological processes of coping (for example, Parkes 1975); the process of role loss that is associated with going from being a member of a couple to being widowed (for example, Blau 1973); and the role and nature of social support (for example, Vachon and Stylianos 1988). These themes are of interest primarily to social scientists rather than to widows. They tell us very little about the world as it confronts older widows in their everyday lives, a void that this book hopes to fill.

Studies on psychological adjustment have concentrated on depressive symptoms (e.g., McCrae and Costa 1988) or emotional distress (e.g., Thompson et al. 1991). As Laurel Smith (1991) has pointed out, much of psychology has also dealt with the pathological consequences and the early stages of widowhood (Haas-Hawkings et al. 1985; Vachon et al. 1982). In fact, it sees grief itself as a pathology (Averill and Nunley 1988).

There has also been an interest in stages of widowhood that are similar to Elisabeth Kübler-Ross's (1969) study on the stages of dying. As early as 1944, Lindemann outlined stages of grieving, and interest in this area of research has continued (e.g., Parkes 1972; Heinemann and Evans 1990). This approach, which began as description, has become prescriptive, an enduring dilemma. With this book, I hope to escape a "stage model" of widowhood, by examining how women respond to very open-ended requests to simply describe their own experiences in their *own* voice.

Researchers who have looked at the social process of role transition have primarily considered the role loss that is involved in the loss of one's husband as simply going from being a wife to being a widow. As Anne Martin Matthews (1991) has pointed out, this fixation on role loss has meant that, apart from a very few studies (e.g., Lopata 1973; van den Hoonaard 1997), no one has examined if and how widows change their sense of self. As we will see throughout this book, women manage to combine developing a redefinition of who they are while maintaining important parts of their identity.

Other studies have looked into the characteristics of widows and have focused on widows' income (Morgan 1986), living arrangements (Fletcher and Stone 1980), etc. This kind of research seems to conceptualize widowhood as an event rather than as a new family stage or a process of transition (O'Bryant and Hansson 1995, 452).

Much of widowhood research has been comparative and has used a survey method. Thus, unlike the current book, many studies only see widows in comparison with other groups rather than as a group worthy of study in their own right. For example, Strykman (1981, cited in Martin Matthews 1991), when considering women's decision to remarry, compares them with men rather than concentrating on the widows themselves. This book endorses Heinemann's (1982) opinion that it is important to study widows in their own right, thus opening the possibility of understanding diversity among older widowed women as well as achieving an in-depth understanding of how they comprehend their own lives.

By using quantitative measures of interaction with both children and friends (e.g., Morgan 1984), most studies reduce an understanding of widows' relationships to a count of how often they see others. As well, researchers have looked at relationships with children in terms of "support" and, therefore, generally only see what the women need from their children rather than what they contribute (O'Bryant and Hansson 1995). In this volume we see the process of negotiation between widows and their children as they redefine their relationships, as well as how expectations can affect a woman's assessment of her relationship with her children—issues we cannot get at simply by counting how many times a week women talk with their children. There are similar drawbacks to literature on widows' relationships with friends and on dating and remarriage.

Even though most widows are old, most literature on widowhood has not studied older persons (O'Bryant and Hansson 1995, 440). An important exception has been Sarah H. Matthews (1979), who used a qualitative method to explore *The Social World of Old Women*. Although Matthews interviewed only widows in the research for her book, the focus of her study was not the experience of widowhood. Arlie Hochschild's (1973) study of older women who live in a subsidized retirement apartment building also involved widows, but did not make widowhood the topic of her study.

Some topics are surprisingly absent in widowhood research. For example, most previous research on widowhood has ignored the role of religion in the life of widows.[4] Helena Lopata (1979), one of the few people who has looked at the place of clergy, has noted that she found little evidence that widows receive help from the clergy. What little other research there is has focused on superficial, countable aspects of the role of religion, for example, frequency of attendance at church (Wortman and Silver 1990). In contrast, because a number of the participants talked about what religion means in their lives, this book includes an in-depth discussion of the role of religion and churches in the lives of older widows.

Finally, beginning with Helena Lopata's groundbreaking study in 1973, most research has involved women who live in large cities. Because the participants in this study live in both urban and rural New Brunswick, we have the opportunity to look at widowhood in the small cities and rural areas where many old people live.

Curiously silent in all of this research on widowhood have been the voices of widows themselves, particularly older widows. We therefore know very little about which issues are important to them. In addition, we have, for the most part, looked only at the negative aspects of widowhood. Thus, we know very little about the more positive things about widowhood as a process of transition, or about the active and dynamic development of relationships that widows engage in as they rebuild their social world (Martin Matthews 1991).

This book is an ethnography that sits on the foundation of symbolic interactionism—a way of looking at the world from the perspective of those being studied. As such, it seeks to describe the system of relationships in which a widow is involved as well as the social processes involved in the negotiation of those relationships (Becker 1996). It recognizes that "all terms that describe people are relational," and that a trait, such as being a widow, is not simply a "fact but rather an interpretation of that fact" (Becker 1998, 132, 134). Hence, symbolic interactionism and qualitative research are the most relevant approaches in the exposition of such social processes.

Howard S. Becker (1996) highlights three important points in the epistemology of qualitative research. First is the insistence on investigating the viewpoints of those studied. The in-depth interview style that I used in the collection of the data that form the subject matter of this book is uniquely designed to encourage study participants to communicate their point of view. The interview asks as few questions as possible and in as broad a way as possible.

The second point Becker raises is the emphasis on the everyday world and everyday life of study subjects. Qualitative research allows people to talk about what happened in their own words. Underlying this practice is the recognition of older widows (in this case) as sentient, experiencing, passionate creatures (Reinharz 1993), who both have an important understanding of their own lives and are capable of telling us about their interpretation of events. It is through focusing on these first two points that we may begin to see older widows' "definition of the situation," which has real consequences for how they live their lives and interpret others' words and actions.

The third point Becker delineates is that ethnography provides a fuller description than variable analysis. This type of work is notable for its breadth. It elucidates a wide range of matters that impinge on the question under study rather than relatively few variables. Thus, this book does not simply look at a few items (i.e., independent variables) to see how they affect a few other items (i.e., dependent variables). Rather, it looks at widows as multidimensional human beings who interact with other individuals, bureaucracies, the memories of their deceased husbands and with themselves in order to understand their everyday lives.

If we sum up the implications of symbolic interactionism as described by Howard S. Becker, we can see that the focus is on meaning rather than rates (W. C. van den Hoonaard 1997, 57). For example, rather than report on how many times a week each participant sees one of her children, a symbolic interactionist concentrates on how older widows talk about their relationships with their children, what those relationships mean to them, how they negotiate those relationships and how all of these things affect their experience as widows.

This theoretical approach seeks to understand social process rather than offer causal explanations (W. C. van den Hoonaard 1997, 58). Instead of simply trying to understand why older widows find it difficult to have friendships—or relationships of any kind—with men, we will examine how they go about trying to interpret men's intentions and how they resolve challenging issues, such as how to interact with married men without the men's wives feeling threatened by the interactions.

Symbolic interactionism also entails an inductive approach, one that seeks to draw theoretical insights along the way that help us understand the data rather than to start with predetermined theoretical assumptions. In this way we do not have to pay the price of allowing a concept to define the case and thereby lose "those aspects of our case that weren't in the description of the category we started with" (Becker 1998, 124). In this way we can continuously add ideas to our collection of data—"the essence of the [interactionist] method" (Becker 1996).

As Anne Martin Matthews has pointed out, "a symbolic interactionist approach is better able to ascertain the basis of responses to bereavement and widowhood and to account for factors that [other theories] cannot adequately consider" (1991, 9). It permits us to achieve some level

of *verstehen*, Max Weber's (1949) term that means to attempt to understand the world from the point of view of those studied (Fine 1990).

This book is organized so that theoretical and conceptual insights
interweave with the data they grow out of. This approach differs from the
more conventional one, where hypotheses, variables, concepts and relevant literature are discussed in advance of presenting the data. Throughout my book, however, the reader will note the continual presentation of
both empirical data and theoretical insights. For example, many older widows take great pride in the fact that they are able to control their emotions when they are with other people and that they are getting on with
their lives rather than wallowing in grief. The concepts of "emotion
work" and "feeling rules" that Arlie R. Hochschild (1979) developed
while studying the commercialization of feeling among airline attendants
helps us to understand the widows' explanations.

Similarly, the concept of "identifying moments," first described by
Kathy Charmaz (1991) in her study of people with chronic illness, sheds
light on how widows state that they suddenly become aware that they are
widows, that their identity has changed. In this way we learn not only specific things about widowhood but about aspects of social processes that
widows share with all people.

From the very first interview, it became obvious that a qualitative and
symbolic interactionist approach resulted in the transcendence of a mech-
anistic view of the experience of becoming a widow, which focuses on
widows as needy, passive individuals. From the first woman's response to
the first question, it became clear that her interpretation of what mattered
about being a widow did *not* start at the moment of her husband's death,
and that women see the transition to widowhood as a process rather than
as a static event.

### Locating the Boundaries of Widowhood

When most of us think of the term widowhood, we feel we know what it
means, that it designates a distinct portion of a person's life that begins
with the death of a spouse. This was certainly my assumption at the
beginning of this study. Even though the published autobiographies I had
read included stories about the deaths of the men who had been married
to the authors, I simply assumed that widowhood begins at the death of
one's spouse, and one's experience is affected by what happens after he
dies: for example, one's level of income or the frequency with which a
widow is in contact with her children. One of the first lessons of this
study was that the way women experience widowhood is not simply con-
tingent on what has happened in that period. Their own understanding

about what is central to that experience includes a much broader definition of what it means to be a widow.

As Phyllis Silverman (1986) notes, one important way to characterize the changes associated with widowhood is to consider what is lost when a spouse dies. She is referring to the roles of husband and wife, both social and legal. Peg[5] let me know immediately that I could not begin to understand her experience as a widow without my understanding what it had been like for her to be a wife:

> What was it like to lose him? I suppose, first of all, you have to say what it was like to have him because that would mean that you have ... he was a very supportive person. He was quite romantic, in a way. We met in a romantic manner ... during the war in London. We did our courting during the Blitz, so he actually saved my life once in the Blitz at some risk to himself. And then he was overseas, too.

Peg took me through a brief history of her marriage and her relationship with her husband. Other women, too, summarized their relationships:

> We, like, were a couple that ... he had his interests and I had my interests. Some of them were the same but we were the type of couple that I would go to a meeting, and he didn't interfere with me going. And when I'd come back, we'd sit in the evenings and talk over what we had done over day time and this I miss very much. That's really the part I miss most of all. (Lydia)

> We were very, very close so that there was nothing that I did that didn't involve him.... We travelled quite a bit when he was able.... That all happened, you see, before I was a widow. So, since I've been a widow ... I just go from one day to the next. There's nothing exciting, really nothing. (Betty)

Sylvia, who had been widowed for the second time, told me that

> He was my mature marriage.... [We] lived for each other, very committed to each other. So it's really been harder this time.

Companionship, financial issues and what couples did together were all aspects of the marriage relationship that women included in their discussion of their experience of widowhood. The details of each component have an important impact on what each woman misses, which aspects of her life are most urgent to rebuild or replace.

Several women told me of an identity so intertwined with their husband's that they were practically one person:

> And he was the focal point of my life as I was of his. So losing him, I kind of lost my compass for quite a while.... You really do become one person. When the other one dies, there's only half left. (Peg)

[The] person [who died] is just an extension of you; you're bonded—all of a sudden there's a void and you have to pick up the pieces and go on. (Muriel)

Helena Lopata (1973) noted this phenomenon of lost identity in the first major study of widowhood in North America. I have not come across one study that did not find the issue of identity central.

But it is not only the relationship that affects a woman's experience of widowhood. The characteristics of her husband himself also contribute a great deal, because it is a particular individual who is missing. For example, Lydia's husband encouraged her participation in various activities:

He was always a great booster, you know. He would always say, "why don't you do it; you can do it." You know, "go ahead and do it." I miss that very much.

Who is there to encourage Lydia now? Other men were described as

a wonderful, happy, gentle man;

a person who shows affection;

such a good man ... a special man ... quite a man;

a man of his family—everything was for us.

Nancy, whose children had made her "promise [she wouldn't] canonize Dad," noted that her husband was "a very happy person." But she continued with:

I have to be careful also when I start expounding his virtues.[6]

This tendency to idealize one's husband crops up frequently in studies of widowhood (e.g., Lopata 1981, 1973).

What is of note is Nancy's awareness of the *danger* and her attempt to circumvent it. It demonstrates her awareness of professional approaches to widowhood. Several other women talked about their experiences in terms of phases or stages and have read self-help books (often given to them by friends). As well, a number attend widowhood support groups. Thus, their experience is also partly defined by what others have told them to expect. As in the area of stages of dying outlined by Kübler-Ross (1969), the experience of widowhood has, to some extent, become prescribed by social scientists as well as described by them.

Women's descriptions of their marriage and what their husband was like begin to tell the story of what their life was like as married women. We begin to see what it is that they have lost. But for many the onset of widowhood was presaged by the illnesses that preceded their husbands' deaths. Hence some included the story of their husband's illnesses as a response to the first question I asked, simply requesting that they talk about their experience as widows. Chapter 1, "The End of the Old Way of Life," provides an in-depth discussion of this ordeal.

Perhaps the most striking example of this is the story of June, the only woman I interviewed whose husband had Alzheimer's disease. Her last years of marriage were defined by the fact that her husband had Alzheimer's disease. She talks about widowhood in terms of the experience of having had her life dominated by this illness and her involvement in the Alzheimer Society.

A number of women answered my first question by talking about the months spent anticipating their husbands' deaths and caring for them. For them, being a widow is partially defined by the care their husbands required as well as anger at hospitals and doctors for either incorrect diagnoses or inadequate care. It is clear that during this period these women's entire lives consisted of caring for their husbands:

> I got so I didn't leave him ... but I didn't mind. I was never involved with anything. (Frances)

Most women are shocked when their husbands die, even if they have been dying for a long time:

> But I don't think you're ever prepared for widowhood.... [My husband] was sick in the hospital for three months so I was alone for those three months, which kind of prepared me to a certain point. But I never really accepted it. (Lydia)

> But it all happened really so fast—I know it was a year, but he was never sick. And it was quite a shock, really. (Edith)

For some women, a long illness allowed them to talk with their husbands about what would happen after they were gone. Part of their experience of widowhood is fulfilling their husbands' expectations, or following their wishes. Some took advantage of this time by doing special things together while their husbands could enjoy them.

Knowing what her husband would want her to do, or spending special time together during illness, has allowed these widows to look at widowhood as continuing their marriage relationship through their actions and reflecting on good memories. Both allow them to view this experience without regret. This is in stark contrast to those whose husbands died suddenly.

What immediately became clear in the reactions of widows to a question that simply asked them to tell about their experience as widows is that the distinction between marriage and widowhood is not always as clear as it would seem. These women do not find the loss of a spouse, in itself, to be meaningful. This loss only makes sense within their own lives when they consider it in terms of what their marriage was like. It is what and who are missing that matters, not what is present. It is this ambiguity that is made visible by letting women tell their own stories (Faraday and Plummer 1970).

As well, the distinction between widowhood and non-widowhood is itself blurred. The experience of their husband's illness and dying, a time when he was still alive, is more an integral part of their experience as widows than it is of their experience as wives. After all, those who were ill for a year or even more were still only ill for a small portion of their marriage. Thus, one woman was able to describe the death of her husband as a shock after an illness of one year.

For some widows, their experience is one of never-ending marriage. This is especially possible for those whose husbands suffered from a long-term illness. In some cases, they were able to ascertain and follow their husbands' wishes for how they should live their lives after his death. They achieve some satisfaction from this continuing relationship. As Kathy Charmaz (1980, 303) has pointed out, in situations like this, the husband remains a "symbolic source of reference ... provid[ing] norms and values ... [and living] on in the subjective experience of the survivor."

Just as locating the boundaries of widowhood turned out to be more complex and subtle than I originally believed, the experiences and interpretations of those experiences of the participants in this study are ambiguous and multifaceted. I have conceptualized these experiences as a journey—a journey with no defined end. This journey sends a woman into a foreign country when her husband dies. Thus, chapter 1 describes the ending of women's old ways of life as their husbands became ill and died.

Chapter 2 describes the beginning of the journey. In the early days, women experience shock and numbness, but retain only a few explicit memories of their husbands' funerals. An abundance of paperwork may add to the confusion of the early days, but it also provides the needed busyness that helps widows get through this difficult time.

Chapters 3 through 5 focus on the efforts of widows to renegotiate their relationships. The old ways of interacting with adult children, friends and men no longer work. These previously straightforward relationships become complicated and filled with unknown dangers they might not anticipate. Their children might treat *them* like children, their friends might desert them and men might misinterpret friendly overtures as invitations to romance. Also unexpected are the new friends and acquaintances widows make as their social circle inexorably changes.

Nonetheless, it is a mistake to assume that all the changes are negative. Growth is also an intrinsic part of widowhood. Thus, chapter 6 looks at areas of growth involved in widowhood. Learning to live alone, to make decisions, to drive and/or to take care of a car are some of the things participants accomplished.

Chapter 7 examines financial issues, which are a challenge that widows must overcome. These include learning how to make important financial decisions and survive on a limited income. Attitudes about money affect relationships with family and friends, and may contribute to the breaking off of contact when jealousy or secrecy are involved.

Chapter 8 looks at the connections participants have to the broader community. It examines what they have said about the place of support groups in their lives, including a six-week workshop, "Striving on Your Own," put on by the Third Age Centre at St. Thomas University, a partner in this study. As well, ties to one's church and one's faith add a potential link to the community. Participation in secular organizations and the world of work adds the last strand.

Finally, the last chapter will summarize the major facets of women's journeys through widowhood and will place these findings in the context of what we already knew about it. It is my hope that by quoting extensively from the widows themselves we can begin to hear their voices, to capture the essence of the journey.

### Notes

1 There are notable exceptions, of course—for example, Sarah H. Matthews's *The Social World of Old Women* (1979) and Arlie Hochschild's *The Unexpected Community* (1973).

2 See Appendix A for a more detailed description of both the sample and the methods I used in collecting the data for this study.

3 The wording of this question was inspired by a report of a study by Riitta-Liisa Heikkinen (1996).

4 In fact, Helena Lopata, in her 1996 book *Current Widowhood: Myths and Realities*, a comprehensive look at what we know about widowhood, and Anne Martin Matthews, in her 1991 book *Widowhood in Later Life*, which recounts the state of the art of widowhood research in Canada, find few studies to cite when they discuss this topic.

5 Unless otherwise stated, all quotations in the book are taken verbatim from the interviews. All the widows' names are pseudonyms, and I have changed minor details when necessary to maintain the confidentiality of the participants.

6 Only two women, including this one, mentioned any problems they had had with their husbands. This woman's husband had had a drinking problem for one part of their marriage.

# Part One

## Embarking on the Journey

—————— *Chapter 1* ——————

# *The End of the Old Way of Life*

Widowhood is an "expectable event" (Martin Matthews 1991) for older women. Nonetheless, when it does come, it usually comes as a shock, whether their husbands were ill for a period of time or died completely unexpectedly. The stories told by the widows I interviewed communicate the emotional depth of the experience of witnessing and sharing in their husbands' deaths. Those whose husbands died after a long illness were often involved in extensive caregiving for their husbands, especially those who either died at home or remained at home until just a few days before their deaths. The knowledge of impending death also gave the couple an opportunity to make the best of the short time left to them and, if their husbands were willing, to talk about the fact that they were dying and what would happen after the death. Judy's sharing of her story exemplifies the unfolding of events.

Judy spoke at length about the time when her husband was ill. Her husband died of cancer (as did many other men whose wives I interviewed). The doctor had predicted that he would have two years to live when he diagnosed the disease. Judy remembers the conversation she had at that time almost word for word:

> So I said ... when he came out to the car, I said, "What did he say?" He said, "Oh, we'll talk about it when we get home." ... So we went home and we sat

—————

Notes to chapter 1 are on pp. 24-25.

down and I made a cup of tea, and he said, "I have cancer." Like that. I, I felt like, you know, I can't move.

At this point Judy and her husband both expected him to recover because "They can get it." Nonetheless, this conversation is burned into her memory, one that she must replay for herself often.

Judy's husband had surgery, which seemed to help, but a year later a CAT scan, in the doctor's words, "lit up like a Christmas tree." Her husband had bone cancer. At this point they began to deal with his impending death. The first conversations they had about this concerned her financial welfare:

> He said, "You know, I have all of my RRIFs[1] in your name. Everything is in your name, all of it."

This involved some joking about what would happen if Judy died first, but as his condition worsened the conversations became more serious:

> As time was getting closer, I would sit with him, and he would say, "Now you'll be all right. You'll be all right." That's what he kept saying.

Finally, Judy's husband requested that he be buried in "consecrated ground" although they had previously bought plots in a Canadian Legion cemetery. She complied with his requests.

Judy imparted these conversations verbatim, an indication that she cherished them. But also of considerable importance was the experience of watching her husband's condition deteriorate and of providing the physical care he required. Strong sentiments of fear and distress at his condition pervade her story:

> But when he got so sick, and he was in such pain, I had to go upstairs because it was so much confusion in the room.... I could hardly sleep because I was up there. So then I had this chair ... in the bedroom, so I could see into the bedroom and ... I spent half my time in a chair ... and I could see him move or ... hear him. And I was giving him morphine ... and I was terrified with that, but the doctor said it was all right.[2]

Judy reports the terrible ambivalence of wanting her husband's suffering to end at the same time as wanting him to live as long as possible:

> I never want to go through anything like that again.... You don't want them to die, and you're saying, "Oh my God, please let him go because he's suffering so much." It's an awful pull one way and the other going.

Extensive caregiving accompanied this suffering. Judy's husband did not want to go into the hospital, so she kept him at home until four days before his death. She did have some help at home from extra-mural nurses[3] and Red Cross homemakers, but "he wouldn't let anybody touch him" except her. Even when he finally entered the palliative care unit in the last few days of his life,

> the nurse said, "He wouldn't let me give him a bath." I said, "What else is new?" ... And I said, "That's all right, I'll do it."[4]

And she did. As difficult as being a widow is for Judy, she comments: "I must say before was much worse than the death."

Nonetheless, as harrowing as these experiences were, they are balanced by special events made possible by the forewarning of her husband's death. For example, she remembers fondly that after his diagnosis her husband insisted that

> "I heard you mention the other day that you wanted another window ... we'll do that." And we went and bought the window early.... So he was thinking all the time—even after [the diagnosis].

Judy is also grateful that she was able to take her husband out to their cottage for his last Thanksgiving. Although others worried about her doing this,

> I said, "He wants to go there and I'm taking him there for Thanksgiving." ... And those friends up there wanted to see him.... So that's what I did. You do what you have to do.

This story contains elements that are common to the stories widows tell about their husbands' period of dying. They include the discovery of their husbands' illness, taking advantage of knowing he was dying, talking about the fact that he was dying, both in terms of the practical "arrangements" and how the widows would continue on with their lives and the experience of caring for their husbands in their final illness.

These women's involvement in the process of dying was profound and important to their experience. Most described without prompting how their husbands had died. The subject arose in response to a variety of questions, including how long they had been married, what it had been like to lose their husbands and where they had been born.[5] This predominance gives a clue to how central the experience was and the fact that memories about their husbands' deaths may never be very far from the minds of these widows.[6]

### The Beginning of the End

Several women pinpointed the moment at which they knew that their husbands were dying. Eleanor's husband had congestive heart failure, which meant that he had to stop working. They moved back to their small hometown and built a retirement home. This "was a dream, to retire and to come home, but it wasn't a dream to come home under the circumstances we came home under." Nancy also painfully related her learning about her husband's illness in terms of a lost retirement together: "we just had a year really or two of comparative retirement." Audrey recalled that her awareness of her husband's impending death had come "on my fiftieth birthday."

Others first became aware that something was wrong when they noticed symptoms that led to the final diagnosis. For example, Polly and her husband, who died of a brain tumour, were on a trip when he suddenly seemed to be

> acting kind of funny ... almost like he wasn't able to process what was being said to him.... I thought ... it was just his age.... But then that evening he did strange things, when we had supper he was trying to cut his meat with his spoon.

And so, New Year's Day saw this couple at the hospital being informed that he had a malignant brain tumour.

Others discovered that their husbands had cancer, but they did not realize that he would die from the disease, or refused to accept that he would not recover:

> But I never really accepted it because I thought when ... they sent him home for two weeks, and I thought, "Oh, great, I'm going to feed him and fatten him up" because he had lost so much weight. And I thought, "This is going to be an excellent summer together." (Lydia)

Lydia and her husband both held out hope for his recovery even when he was days from death. She pointed out that, in order to get admitted to the palliative care unit at the hospital, they had to "accept this thing." Outwardly they went along with the doctor. But Lydia believed that

> where there's life there's hope and I lived in the hopes that [my husband] would perhaps get better and truly we never talked about death, he and I.[7]

Emily, on the other hand, was particularly upset, because she felt that had she known the seriousness of her husband's illness they would have been able to prepare for his death:

> So, had we known he had such little time, and I said that at the time, we will take the summer and do things we would have wanted to. He wouldn't have worked every day.

In contrast, a number of those who, like Judy, knew their husbands were dying, are grateful that they had the time to do special things with their husbands at the end of their lives. Martha recounts the last summer she and her husband had together:

We spent our time together, well day and night.... I took him out a lot for drives.... He seemed to enjoy the summer.

Peg states that

We realized that our time was short. So we made the best of it. We really did. We did some trips and enjoyed ourselves. And probably had the most serene and really loving kind of relationship ... that we had ... stretched out over all the ups and downs of marriage before. So that it was a time that was given to us especially.

Lydia and her husband managed to make their weekly one-hour trips for treatment into a special time:

We travelled to ____ and back and it was nice because it was a lovely summer too, and we enjoyed it and we always liked to travel in the car.

Being able to take advantage of having advance notice of their husbands' deaths depended to some extent on their husbands' willingness to talk about the fact that they were, in fact, dying. Several women reported that their husbands had not been willing to talk about the fact that they were dying. For example, Sarah commented that her husband "knew, but never said [that he was dying]." Marilyn and her husband did not have "long discussions," but she felt that "he was entitled to handle it whatever way he wanted to."

Polly, on the other hand, found it frustrating that her husband would not talk to her about things:

He would not talk about it at all. I couldn't get him to tell me, you know, make plans or anything.... I tried to talk to him about who would you like to give this to and who would you like to give that to and he just, he just wouldn't talk to me at all.

Others who did not talk with their husbands about their death commented that they "were waiting to be ready" (Doris) when time ran out unexpectedly. Blanche stated that for a long time her husband "was always hopeful that ... this would help or that would help." By the time it became obvious to him, "he was in such pain that he really couldn't talk."

Audrey's husband initially did not want to talk about the fact that he was dying, but the extra-mural nurses, who were helping her care for her husband at home, encouraged her to confront him directly with her need to talk about the fact that he was dying:

And that worked very well.... I think he was afraid to talk, he wanted to talk about it, but he was afraid because he didn't want to upset me and yet I had to know, too. And when I did that then after that he would talk a lot.

Those who did have conversations with their husbands about their impending deaths talked about his will (Judy) and instructions regarding his funeral and burial or cremation (Judy, Marilyn, Eileen). More valuable were conversations about the widow's future. Eileen's husband, for example, consoled her by telling her that her daughters would be there for her:

> He always said to me ... "You have your girls, don't worry, everything, everything is going to be all right."

Martha's husband, on the other hand, wanted her to reassure him that she'd be all right:

> He used to say, "I worry about you, how you're going to make out." And I just said, "Listen, you don't worry about me, right now our concern is you, keeping you comfortable and content." And he was very content.

But as his death approached he told her that she was to go on with her life. Martha repeats this conversation word-for-word:

> About two weeks before he died ... he woke up and he looked at me, and I was sitting there, and he said, "Do you want to talk?" I said, "Sure, I'd love to talk." So I went over and sat on the edge of his bed beside him, and he said, he looked up at me and he said, "I want you to go on with your life." And I said, "Oh?" "Yes, I don't want you sitting in the house and moping around. I want you to get out and enjoy yourself." I said, "Well, I'll make out fine, dear." I said, "Our daughters will look after that." So he went right back to sleep, that was all he could say.

In contrast, Peg's husband worried that she would remarry:

> "You're waiting until I die, and then you're going to get married again." I said, "... there's no way in the wide world that I would ever marry anybody again.... We're going to shake hands on it ... because there's no way." I said, "You just wait for me wherever you go; I'll be there." And we shook hands on it, and he felt better after that.

Eileen's husband reported seeing a partially open door with a bright light on the other side. This gave her warning that he would die very soon. Marie's husband comforted her by assuring her that he was "at peace." This was especially significant, because she had to make the heart-rending decision to order the doctor

> to disconnect everything you've got.... There was no point. That was one thing he had made me promise, "If I ever be like this don't do anything for me. I want to go in peace." ... Oh my God, this is the worse ... thing to see, really. To say to take the bottles down ... it is a terrible, terrible thing. It's almost like you take a gun and you shoot somebody ... an hour later he was dead.

### *Taking Care: The Best of Times ... The Worst of Times*

For many, witnessing their husbands' deaths is not simply a matter of passively hoping that he might recover while waiting for him to share his feelings. Rather, they take an active role in caring for their husbands as their physical condition deteriorates. This caregiving entails love, fear and sorrow.[8]

For Marilyn and Polly this necessitated spending innumerable hours in the hospital. Marilyn communicated vivid memories of frustration:

> I was there every day with him for usually twelve hours.... I fought for everything he needed and wanted. It was just a constant battle.

This frustration was eased when her husband finally entered the Palliative Care Unit, which was "fantastic." Polly was more satisfied with the care her husband received in hospital, but she recounted going back and forth to the hospital every weekend.

Others took care of their husbands at home. For most this was either their husbands' or their preference, but when I asked Blanche if this had been a good decision, she remarked simply that she had not been given any choice, and

> I found it quite distressing trying to sort of feed him these things which he couldn't take.

Even more disturbing was the sign on her refrigerator which read:

> "No Resuscitation." ... You sort of have to pass this notice every time you went into the kitchen.... The nurses were extremely kind and helpful. But it was tough, it was tough.

The sign was there to prevent attempts at resuscitation in the event that an ambulance had to be called. No matter how sick Blanche's husband got,

> Nobody said, "Oh, he's so sick ... he better go to hospital."

She maintains that she is still "getting over the last week" of her husband's life.

Others focused on the struggle of taking care of a loved one at home. For example, Lydia noted that she had never wanted to be a nurse, but in caring for her husband at home discovered that she could do things she never thought she could. This is a real accomplishment for Lydia, but she points out that the last two weeks of her husband's illness were

> the worst two weeks of my life.... [You are] left on your own ... scared to death.

Eileen also focused primarily on the challenges she faced:

I had him here at home. I took care of him until he died.... It's not easy to
see a loved one deteriorate before your eyes.

Others seemed more content with the experience, seeing it less as an
ordeal than another opportunity to demonstrate their love for their
husbands.[9] Frances, in her mid-eighties, for example, kept her husband
with her at home against the advice of her doctor who said:

"I hope you know what you're doing." ... It would not have been any easier
on me [if my husband had been in a nursing home] because he would have
expected me to go [visit] and how could I go to a nursing home?

Sarah recalled warmly that with her husband home, "he was close when I
was doing anything," while Peg was glad that she could "stay with him
twenty-four hours a day."

Audrey's story captures the emotional struggle combined with the
accomplishment of succeeding in taking care of her husband at home:

And I remember the last week, too, when they brought in the oxygen, and
they had this computer thing for the pain medication.... And I never wanted
to be a nurse ... I said, "No way—that wasn't my thing and here all this stuff
in here" ... and [my minister] came in and I said, "... I think I've got to put
him in the hospital, you know. I can't handle all this stuff." And he said,
"No, Audrey, he doesn't want to go to the hospital." ... And, of course,
afterwards I was so thankful that I hadn't weakened.

In the end, she concluded, "it's so much easier with them home because
you're there twenty-four hours a day.... It's just when ... the room
becomes a hospital" that things seem overwhelming.

Inevitably, their husbands died. For several of the women whose husbands were able to remain at home, it was extremely important that they
were there when their husbands did finally die. For both Sarah and
Eleanor, it is comforting to know that their husbands died peacefully in
their arms. Eleanor tenderly recalls the last moments of her husband's life:

A very peaceful death for him.... He wasn't aware of anything.... We had
gone to bed later on a Friday night ... and we were laying there, and he had
his arm under my pillow and his other arm around me.... About five minutes
before, he had ... said, "I love you so much." And then he said, "I've got to
move." And I said, "Have I got your arm pinched?" ... And he said, "No,
I'm dizzy." And that was it.

Eileen also recounts a gentle moment right before her husband's
death that would not have occurred had she not had the courage to remain
with him until the end:

I didn't think I was going to be able to be in the room when he died. But when he started, that morning when he couldn't open his eyes and he was breathing harshly ... I started to pray, and I figured, "That's it," and then I held his hand, and I said to him, "The Lord is waiting for you. He's waiting for you. It's okay to go, I'll be all right." He just gave me a tight squeeze and let go. That was it.... I guess God gives you strength.

Sharon also recounts her husband's dying immediately after being "given permission" to let go, and Judy's husband seemed to be able to hang on until she arrived at the hospital to say good-bye.

It is clear from the above accounts that being able to be with one's husband at the point of death can provide a special moment from which widows may derive some comfort. The fact that a number of them can provide a word-by-word account without hesitation illustrates the centrality of this event. For others, *not* being present when their husbands died produced a painful memory. It is with a sense of irony that Emily, Betty and June point out that well-meaning loved ones had encouraged them to go home and rest on the night that turned out to be the last night of their husbands' lives. Betty's story, for example, captures the distress she still feels at not being at the hospital when her husband died:

They had [my husband] in a private room, and they said they'd bring in a bed for me, and [my son] objected to that. He said, "I don't think so, Mom.... You should go home. We'll stay here overnight and you'll feel better in the morning, to come back, than you will if you sit here all night." So I said, "Will you stay right here?" ... I didn't think he was gonna die like that.... So I went home and I laid down on the couch. And I must have gone to sleep all right, and the next thing the phone rang and it was [my son], and he said, "Dad's gone."

Nonetheless, the regret felt by those who were not there when their husbands died after a long illness does not compare with the feelings of those whose husbands died suddenly.

### No Chance to Say Good-bye

And we were both in the K-Mart, and he was buying little gifts for my [Christmas] sock and I was going to get some things, and I said, "Look ... I'll meet you." ... And last I seen him bouncing around.... When I came out there was a big crowd out there, and I looked around and somehow I did not even see him, but I knew it was him ... I felt it. He was laying on the floor. They had cut his coat off, down the front, and they were giving him CPR.... I can still see his face, so black, just so black. (Sharon)

The horror and shock of sudden death seems alive with every telling of the story. Often this is accompanied by obsessively trying to relive that day or those days in ways that might change what happened in some respect. For example, Sharon's son had called the morning of his father's heart attack to suggest that he come for a visit that morning. She turned him down and, in her mind, this resulted in his missing a final opportunity to see his father. Sylvia feels guilty because, when her husband collapsed, "stupid me, I didn't realize how very serious it was.... I should have."

In contrast, although Marion did say that her husband's sudden death was "kind of a shock," she was relieved that he did not go through a long period of declining health:

> It was good because he had a terrible fear of being in a nursing home and having a long period where he was disabled.

A few women whose husbands had become ill suddenly did feel that their death was at least partially a result of the mismanagement or misdiagnosis by hospital staff. For example, Cathy insists that

> they were treating [my husband] more for indigestion than anything. But it turned out it was the aorta.... They came running with Maalox for him.

Whether their husbands died suddenly or after a long illness, whether they were with their husbands when they died or whether they were sent home, at the end of the process these women are now all widows. In the next chapter we will see what the first days of widowhood were like.

## Notes

1 An RRIF is a Registered Retirement Income Fund. This is one of the tax deferral savings plans that encourage savings by taxing income when it is paid out after retirement when people are usually in lower tax brackets than when they were working. "Taxes are only paid on the money received each year" (National Council on Welfare 1996, 41).

2 Several women talked about the experience of giving their husbands morphine while caring for them at home. This led to his sleepiness and disorientation, and for most was a disturbing experience. They knew the effects of the drug, were frightened by it and knew that it meant the end was near.

3 New Brunswick has an extra-mural hospital which provides nursing assistance in the home and, therefore, allows people to remain there rather than enter the hospital. It "was established ... in 1981 as a planned response to a combination of forces.... [It] provides [professional and support services] only to those who can be *safely* cared for at home.... The aim is to provide a continuum of high quality care while treating [its] patients with dignity, sympathy and consideration—as people rather than inanimate objects on a conveyor belt of impersonal care" (The New Brunswick Extra-Mural Hospital, n.d.; emphasis in original). All the women I interviewed, who had had the services of the extra-mural hospital, praised the care and dedication of the nurses. Audrey made the point that in a hospital the staff cares only for the patient while the extra-mural nurses care for the whole family.

4 Peter Townsend (1957, 56-57), in his classic study of old people's family life in Great Britain, noted this disinclination towards anyone but a spouse providing "bodily care.... The care of a man's body was felt to be the prerogative of his wife and it was thought to be a break with propriety if [anyone else were] to undertake such an intimate task."

5 In fact, I had originally planned to ask how the husbands had died, but eventually took it out of the interview schedule because it was unnecessary. This is in contrast to the findings of Helena Lopata (1979, 103) in her classic study of widows in Chicago. She commented: "There is a tendency for the widow not to report involvement in the circumstances of her husband's death, less than half making some reference to their own actions.... All in all, there are few women who feel that they might have been able to do something constructive to prevent the death or assist the dying."

6 Howard S. Becker (1970) suggests that volunteered statements have greater "evidentiary value" than those directed by the interviewer. If this is the case, then these women's desire to recount the "death stories" of their husbands cannot be ignored.

7 Perhaps it was this optimism that allowed her and her husband to interpret their trips for chemotherapy as pleasant.

8 This section does not include the caregiving experiences of June, whose husband had Alzheimer's disease. This entailed eight years of looking after him at home, followed by daily visiting at a nursing home. See the work of Hazel MacRae (1995) for a sensitive and insightful analysis of the experiences of family caregivers of Alzheimer's victims.

9 Motenko (1988) reports that older men who care for disabled wives also report feelings of pride that they are able to care for and show love to their wives.

# Chapter 2

# The Journey Begins

**W**hether he dies suddenly or after a lengthy illness, when a woman's husband dies her world changes in fundamental ways. She experiences strong reactions, both emotional and physical. Paradoxically, she feels numb while, at the same time, she has strong emotional reactions to the things people do and say. Everything that happens becomes magnified. Therefore, the actions of others, positive or negative, are remembered clearly and retain importance. In addition to the highly charged emotional atmosphere surrounding events immediately following a husband's death is the need to be very busy—both in response to necessary paperwork and as a way of dealing with these struggles. The following pages will look at how the widows who participated in this study remembered those very difficult first days.

The most common response to my question regarding what stood out most vividly from the first few days after their husbands' deaths was "shock." Those whose husbands had died unexpectedly report being both shocked and in a daze:

> I guess it's all for the shock ... it's so unbelievable ... really too much. I just couldn't believe it, you know, it was so unbelievable. (Cathy)

> At first you're kind of numb ... overwhelmed. (Marion)

Notes to chapter 2 are on pp. 40-41.

You're more or less in shock when they die like that. (Florence)

Those whose husbands' deaths were expected, however, also expressed a feeling of shock and, sometimes, bewilderment:

I guess when death occurs, you go into a bit of a shock, which carries you through all that more or less. (Marilyn)

Oh, I would say numbness, absolute numbness.... I was just stunned, numb. (Lynn)

Blanche's comment conjures up the sense of detachment from those around her that results from the intensity of the experience:

It's a ... total shock to the system.... I found it was like being indoors and looking through thick glass at the world outside. You could see it, but you weren't sort of there. Even to go shopping, you could see the things on the shelves, but you're sort of not there.... Of course, you sort of know you're there, but you don't feel as if you're there.

Judy's and Edith's shock was so great that they cannot remember anything about those first few days, and Emily still shudders to remember

getting in the car and driving and not know[ing] where I am. I'd be some place and wonder how I got there.

Although so many of these women spent months caring for their husbands and expressed such sorrow at seeing them suffer, only one, Audrey, voiced a sense of relief:[1]

I remembered just going through the motions. But there was that relief, you know, no question.

Shock also manifests itself in physical reactions. Both Frances and Martha remember feeling cold and shaky. Peg felt as if she had sustained a mortal wound. Cathy and Eileen recall crying a great deal while Eleanor's first reaction was "screaming, screaming, screaming."

Three women describe a feeling of no longer being a whole person. For example, Martha said:

I said, "Now, it's so final." I just feel that I've lost a part of me ... and I still do feel a part of me went.

Peg puts it this way:

I kind of lost my compass.... I think anybody who has been together that long; you really do become one person.... There's only half of you left.[2]

The shock is so overwhelming that some women find it very difficult to realize what has actually happened. Nancy admitted that it didn't register for a while. Both Edith and Marie coped the first few days by pretending that their husbands had not, in fact, died. Edith recalls:

> The only way I got through those first few days, I think, was to keep thinking that [my husband] was in hospital. I wouldn't let myself believe that he was gone.

Marie pretended to herself that her husband was on one of his occasional trips overseas. This reluctance to admit her husband was dead was so strong that even several months later, when I was speaking with her, she commented:

> I'm starting now to say, "He's not gone [overseas]; he's not coming back."[3]

Nonetheless, although many women feel out of control in the first days after their husbands have died, several remember making attempts to quickly "put on a good front" (Doris, Edith) or to "pull myself together" (Lydia). Even Marie, whose husband died suddenly and who was still trying to come to grips with the reality of his death months later, remarked that in the first days after his death, it had fallen to her to be "the strong one."

Paradoxically, feelings of numbness and shock are accompanied by strong emotional reactions to what people are doing or saying. Edith and Judy remember being very angry at doctors and the hospital, while Marie reports feeling angry at her husband. But it is the actions, both positive and negative, of those surrounding these widows right after their husbands' deaths that continue to resonate for them.

Although there has been a decrease in the ritual surrounding a death (Gorer 1965), being surrounded by people remains a common experience for new widows. The women who participated in this study were very moved by what they perceive as an outpouring of love and affection for their husbands during the few days following their deaths. When I asked about Sharon's most vivid memories after her husband's death, she replied:

> Perhaps shock and overwhelmed with the love that I got from people. As I stood in the undertakers ... I thought, "I'm not going to be able to cope with this crowd." I looked out the door and it was clear down to the street, the people, and I thought, "Oh this, is, I cannot shake hands ..." but somehow something came over me, and I went right through it and I enjoyed that, if you can enjoy something like that.... It was such a touching feeling that so many people.... (Sharon)

This image of people lined up all the way down the street is not an uncommon one. Eleanor remembers that "hundreds of people came through," while for Martha, who recollects that not everybody who came to the visitation at the funeral home could get in because of the crowds, the symbol of that support is that

> [The Mayor] came three times before he got in. He had meetings and he said, "I had to go back to the meetings." Then he'd come back and it would still be lined to the road.... He came back three times before he got in.

June remembers the reception put on by friends, while Lydia recalls the amount of food brought by members of a sororal organization.

Widows often interpret this expression of support and/or affection as an indication of the high esteem in which their husbands were held by colleagues and friends. This provides comfort and is very meaningful. For Sarah, for example, this was the most striking thing about her first few days as a widow:

> I think it was the people that came, and the stories they told, and told me how much they loved my husband. I mean, I knew he was liked, but I didn't know he was liked so much or had so many friends. I think that would be the most.

Indeed, there is ample evidence that, for most women, the presence of many people eased them through those early days. Betty provides a contrasting reaction. She wanted to have only her children around right after her husband died. Rather than seeing the company of many people as comforting, she saw it as an intrusion:

> And we got back home here, and the minister and I were in the kitchen. The rest of them were all inside, and people, that we asked *not* to come, came.... And I didn't want to talk to anybody. I just wanted my kids around.... And they were buzzing around here in the kitchen.... I went straight to the bathroom. I didn't want to see anybody.... But I had to come out and sit in the living room with these strange people ... around.... And the whole thing is a *horror campaign*, and if I had my way, there wouldn't *be any of that* [emphasis in original].

Others had similarly strong reactions to being left alone right after their husbands died. Frances, who showed very little emotion for most of the time I was with her, for example, was moved to tears by the memory of spending the first night after her husband died alone. Marion also spent the first night alone and

> afterwards I felt a little resentful that no one was here.... You go through all the difficult times alone.

It is clear that, although people have individual desires about what should happen in the first few days, their reactions to whether or not things went as they should have are strong and long-lasting. These women have comparable reactions to the support or lack of support they felt from their children during these first few days.

Emily, for example, warmly recalled her son's saying to her:

> "Mom, I hope that someday I find a girl, that we're in love as much as, you know, the way that you and Dad were as good for each other."

Both Lynn's and Cathy's children wrote moving tributes to their fathers. Cathy still brings her daughter's letter to her father out to remind herself how much her children loved their father, and she also brought the letter out for me to read.

Equally significant are problems with family that arose during the first few days of these women's widowhood. Not least were issues associated with stepchildren. Judy's thoughts turn to the shock of having her stepchildren seem to turn against her because her husband had left her RRIFs in his will. Florence recounted a convoluted tale that seemed to be related to a stepgranddaughter's efforts to blackmail her as she had been blackmailing Florence's husband.

For June, the problem with her son and his family was a continuation of the estrangement that she feels was part of her son's discomfort being around his father when he had Alzheimer's disease. Nonetheless, the memory is still painful and embarrassing:

> Well, it was very hard for me because I have a son in Alberta.... They came, but they didn't even have jackets for the [teenaged] boys. The boys didn't even have a suit on, they just had jeans and a shirt, you know, to the funeral, his father's funeral.... They went back right after the funeral. They never even drove back over here to see my daughter.... So that hurt a lot with my son.

June's relationship with her son remains distant.

### The Funeral

The funeral is the central ritual surrounding death, but most women do not have extensive recollections about this ritual. The most prominent memory about their husbands' funeral is the number of people who attended it. If that number exceeded their expectations, they were "overwhelmed" with how many were there. Just as we have the strong visual image of people lined up into the street during visitation before the funeral, we have a similarly evocative picture of chapels overflowing with those attending the funeral:

> My husband was a special man.... When we had a memorial mass for him ... I catered for about three hundred people, I thought about three hundred peo-

ple would come to the reception ... and it was 950 people.... My church ... seats a thousand, and there wasn't a pew to be had. So it touched more people than I thought.... He must have touched a lot of people. (Eileen)

And:

Oh, it was overflowing. It was just in the funeral parlour.... They had to open everywhere, all the rooms in there because it was packed, it was packed ... and I was really surprised, not expecting that at all, not at all. (Marie)

In addition to the unexpectedly large funeral noted by eight of the women I interviewed was the gratifying surprise of particular individuals who unexpectedly showed up and gave the widows a sense that their husbands' memories were cherished. Sarah was very moved by:

One little boy, I just still can't get over it. It was a child that I'd taught in school.... He used to come down here on a Saturday.... He came to funeral and he cried and he cried.... He said, "He was the only father I ever knew." ... And it's people like this and like that girl coming from Halifax and saying, "He's like my father." We didn't know this when he was alive.

Martha was amazed that nurses who had cared for her husband thought enough of him to come to his funeral:

And that meant a lot to me, just to see those two girls, you know.

However, not everybody had a large funeral. Marion's husband wanted no funeral and had none.

Betty reported similar distaste for her husband's funeral as she had for the people who had come to her home after his death. She acknowledges that some people prefer large funerals, but she would have liked her wishes to have been honoured:

It's nothing but a hell. Maybe some people liked it, but I sure didn't. It's something they put the family through for somebody's looks. You know, there's a lot of people that [like] to have all these showy things.

So, again, while most women interpreted large attendance as an outpouring of affection and caring, Betty had a more cynical view.

The women in this study did not have strong memories surrounding the making of arrangements for their husband's funeral. Only a few of the men had left specific instructions or had discussed plans with their wives. For the most part, the women were helped by their children or left the entire job of arranging the funeral to their children.

Canada's climate adds an unwanted wrinkle to making burial arrangements if death occurs in the winter when the ground is frozen. Mimi and

Marilyn found having to wait until spring to bury their husbands and, thus, to go through the funeral twice, very difficult.

The scattering of ashes lent another challenge for some of the widows. Marion, several years after her husband's death, was still trying to locate an appropriate spot, while Blanche confided that she and her children had scattered the ashes in her backyard and planted a tree as a marker.

In recent years there has been some movement from the idea of a funeral as a memorial to a funeral as a celebration of the life of the person who has died. This trend had a limited effect on this group of women. Two, Lynn and Audrey, described their husband's funeral in this way. For example:

> It was a celebration of [my husband's] life, not a funeral.... It must be all joyful and bright and upbeat. And it was. (Lynn)

Once the funeral is over, one begins to deal with the enormity of what has happened. One way of handling this is to keep busy.

### Keeping Busy

Immediately after an adult dies, the survivor has a large amount of paperwork to deal with, and these women were no exception. There are countless forms regarding pensions, bank accounts, credit cards, car registration, etc. Some funeral homes do provide a packet of forms to the widow, but some women are so stunned by their husbands' deaths that they have no memory of receiving such a packet. Blanche recalls "being flooded with paper," and Marion comments that she became involved in "a frenzy of activity" surrounding the paperwork that needed to be done. Many were surprised at how much there was to look after. Marie said that she "couldn't believe it." But it is important to remember that this is all taking place at a time when many are not thinking clearly. Judy's remarks are telling:

> There's so many things you have to do when your husband dies, I couldn't believe it.... I was fortunate and I had a brother that just kind of took over for me. And afterwards I thought, "Gee, I didn't do all those things." ... I didn't even know I had to make out an estate tax.... I would never have done it. They probably would have had me in jail. I never would have thought of it.... It was amazing.

Others did the paperwork on their own and found it onerous:

> And it was a lot of paperwork. I couldn't believe all the paperwork that existed.... It's hard because you have to think of everything. (Marie)

Lynn spent two weeks doing nothing but paperwork, and she listed what had been required:

> I was down here changing this document, getting my birth certificate.... My ... car registration changed ... changing my own will, getting another power of attorney, doing all these legal things ... wresting investments out of what he had.... That's what I did during the first two or three weeks. Busy, busy, busy, busy.

Dealing with bureaucracy can be frustrating, as Marilyn pointed out to me at length, but this enforced busyness also helps the women deal with the overpowering emotional adjustment they are facing:

> It's all these little things that get you ... little details and you know, but you get through it. Maybe it helps you.... Maybe when you have so much to do, it helps you. (Sarah)

Many people give widows advice about how to deal with the adjustment to being a widow. One of the more common pieces of advice is to keep busy, and not only did people give these widows that advice, but many of them agreed that keeping busy is crucial.

Several women describe keeping busy as a way to deal with particular aspects of coping with their situation. Emily

> took my frustrations out in my door yard, like my flowers ... started a flower garden and mowing the lawn and stuff like that.

Martha found evenings particularly difficult so she

> Made quilts ... and crocheted some on an afghan, finished up one and started another one. And I just ... kept busy with things in the evenings because the evenings were very long.

Peg's family immediately set out on a program to "keep Grandma busy," and Doris remembers that as the first piece of advice she received:

> I think it was my sister said, "Well, keep as busy as you can." ... That is so true because I found if I was with someone else, I was much less apt to sit and think.

June, whose husband had Alzheimer's disease, had spent the last several years doing extensive caregiving and going back and forth to the nursing home in the little while preceding his death. Thus, busyness had become an integral part of her life. As a result:

> I didn't know just what to do with myself.... So I just worked more with patients.... I still go down there every day and help feed the patients.

Keeping busy is a way of surviving, and for Eleanor it has become a way of life that began when her husband died and continues:

But one thing, from the minute [my husband] died until the present, I have kept myself so busy that sometimes I wonder if I keep too busy.... I don't know if I can cope with being home alone.... I have stayed so busy that I ... guess I program myself that way. I keep thinking, "What am I supposed to be doing now?"

Three of the women whom I interviewed are still in the workforce, and each used going back to work as a way of managing. Each went back to work quickly, more quickly than others might have deemed appropriate. Marion recalls:

I just went back to work.... I went back to work [three days later].... Everybody at work was a little bit shocked to see me in there. But they just sort of left me alone and it seemed to be okay.... I just carried on the way I always had ... just appearing normal.

Marie explicitly remarks that going back to work was, for her, the way to keep busy:

I went back to work the week after he was buried, but I thought it would be better.... And people reproached me on that. Some people.... I had to keep busy.... I couldn't stand being alone in the house.

Audrey, who teaches adults, also "stayed off a week." She worried about the awkwardness she and her students might feel, but

I was really warmed by my students' response.... It gave me strength.

Florence interprets this press to keep busy as a natural part of the mourning process that everybody has to go through. She feels it is a way you heal from the shock of losing your husband both physically and emotionally:

Now there's a shock that goes into your system, and ... your body has to heal from that.... You just feel as though you're right out straight continually.... You just feel as though you're just racing.

One task that confronts most women is dealing with the condolence cards and letters they receive. Nancy said that she "set [herself] the task of answering all the cards and letters" as a way of keeping busy. But this correspondence is more than simply a way of making time pass; it also provides a source of comfort that is enduring for many women.

### Cards and Letters

The cards and letters widows receive in response to their husbands' deaths are most notable for their message that people cared for and about their husbands. They reinforce the belief that these men were special and good men. They elicit an especially powerful reaction when they come from unexpected people or in great numbers. As well, as Doris pointed out, receiving a card from "someone who has been widowed ... [and] knows how I feel" can be very helpful.

Eileen quoted from letters that referred to her husband as "our teddy bear." She remembers that younger "girls" from "down home" were very fond of her husband and would hug him when they saw him at church. She was touched when they wrote to her:

> Well, we lost our teddy bear.

Lydia was very moved at the number of cards and letters she received, more than two hundred, while both Blanche and Eileen were moved by cards and messages that came from unexpected quarters. In the case of Blanche a handwritten note from a car dealership made an impression. Eileen was very surprised when

> I [got] notes and letters from people that ... he had worked with, and he had helped with.... I didn't even know—he did all this in silence. He was quite ... a man.

Several women find comfort in rereading these letters and notes and keep them around for that purpose. Sharon received a letter from her minister that

> If I feel a bit down, I read it over.... He wrote the nicest letter ever.... He wrote pages to me.... It [would be] just worth you reading it, the wording in it, the comfort. Like one place he puts in it, "I have tried to put myself in your place if my wife died, but there's no way I can." ... And I thought, he took the time to write this beautiful letter.

She has reread this letter so many times that she has actually memorized portions of it. Emily also noted that she keeps the letters in a basket where she can easily reread the letters that are most important to her.

A letter from her daughter has been particularly important for Cathy, who finds that daughter impatient with her mourning for her husband. She pulls that letter out and rereads it to remind herself how much her daughter loved her father.

Lynn remarked that she now understands how important these cards can be. Whereas before her husband died, she might have meant to send a card and forgotten, now she

> will do it.... I will do it because it was a very important thing ... and I see it is very important to others, too.

This significance is underlined for Lynn by her strong reaction to not receiving a card from people she thought were very good friends.

The funeral, the necessary paperwork and the condolence cards and letters all serve as reminders that widows have entered a new stage in their lives, that of being widows. But for many, this realization suddenly comes upon them and hits them hard. The next section will look at how women describe this "identifying moment,"[4] and what acknowledging that they are widows means to them.

### *I Am a Widow*[5]

All but a few women were able to pinpoint when and how they had realized that the term widow now refers to them. Whether they realized it immediately (Lynn, Florence) or whether it hit them after a time, at some point most had to accept their new status and begin to integrate it into their sense of who they are.

The most common response to my question about how they first came to think of themselves as widows was that they told themselves that they were widows. Lynn said:

Oh, you think of yourself as a widow immediately.

Similarly Florence insisted:

As soon as they die, you think of it, you say you're a widow.

For Cathy it was a matter of thinking, "I guess I'm alone now; I must be a widow or something."

Some women report that their realization was sudden and shocking. The suddenness of that realization is what Eleanor feels most strongly:

All of a sudden it occurred to me, "I am a widow." Even though my mail may come as Mrs. _____, I am a widow.... And it was like all of a sudden I realized it.... It hadn't occurred to me ... at the time of death or at the funeral ... just all of a sudden, it hit me, "Hey, I am a widow."

Polly does not remember when, but that at some point it just "hit me." Audrey was amazed to hear herself refer to herself as a widow in response to someone's question:

Somebody asked me something, and I said, "Oh, I'm a widow." And it really shocked me. 'Cause all of a sudden there it was, and it was real.

Four women felt this same sense of sudden awareness of their new state when they were filling out a form. Nancy, for example, had felt she was doing pretty well until she had to sign papers for which she had to assert that she was a widow. That was when it "hit me." Blanche also realized she was a widow when she had to note her marital status on a form "for the first time, and that's very hard."

This unexpected nature of realization meant that it could come at any time. For Sharon it came as a total surprise when someone referred to her as a widow:

> It hit me so hard, it almost turned me sick for the moment. Somebody said, "You're a widow." And it almost made me feel sick to my stomach. That was the first time—I had never thought of myself as being a widow.

This happened several months after Sharon's husband died. She

> kind of had a resentment feeling.... As much to say, "who do they think they are telling me I'm a widow all of a sudden?"

Regardless of what set off their identifying moment, most women had a fairly clear idea of the image conjured up by the term "widow." The three most common associations were that widows are "old," "alone" and "on their own."

Nancy, for example, feels that calling someone a widow is the same as saying you're old. A few women felt that the term was more appropriate to refer to someone older than themselves. Doris was reluctant to use the word to refer to herself because

> As long as you don't use the term, maybe you can say it doesn't apply to me yet.

Doris thinks of a widow as "some[one] very older, a much older woman and more dependent."

This reaction is not surprising for the women in their fifties. Audrey commented that one usually thinks of a widow as being an "old lady," and Marion noted that "a lot of widows are older than I am. I felt young to be a widow.' Marie stated categorically:

> I'm too young. I feel that I'm too young to be a widow. A widow is ... older.... I feel too young to be a widow. It's, a widow to me is if you're eighty and over ... if you're older than that.

Her feelings are so strong that she does not use the word widow to refer to herself.

For some, accepting the fact that they are widows means realizing that they are now alone. The terms "widow "and "alone" are almost synonymous. For example, when I asked Muriel when she first thought about herself as a widow, she responded:

> It was wasn't too long after he passed away. Here I am, I'm alone.

Doris also remembers consciously telling herself:

> "You are alone now. You do not have someone else's support." And I ... used to have to tell myself that quite often at the beginning.

Eleanor's comments summon up images of abandonment:

I have nobody. I am alone.... I feel, you know, there's only me.

The overwhelming sense of aloneness combines, for some, with a realization that they are on their own, that they have to learn to take care of and do things for themselves. For example, Lydia tied the two images together:

Well, I think of a person who's strictly alone ... who has to be very self-reliant now.... I'm the only one, you know, I have to make all the decisions.

Similarly, Eleanor realized that "all the decisions are yours now," while Muriel commented:

I have to be an independent person. I have to make my own way.

In contrast, Emily and Doris envisage a widow in terms of dependence:

Somebody's got to look after me, type of thing. (Emily)

A much older woman and a much more dependent person than I felt I was. (Doris)

Marion thinks of widows as leading "a restricted life." Other connotations that came up during this discussion were that widows are "staid and exemplary" (Nancy), "careful around men of other wives" (Sharon) and "diminished." (Peg)

It is important to keep in mind that these connotations of widowhood were not necessarily the way the women look at themselves. They recognize the stigma that is attached to the word "widow," and, therefore, many are reluctant to apply the term to themselves because they do not resemble what they feel is the typical widow and, as Emily comments, see that in some ways they feel that simply taking on the label diminishes them:

I still don't like that word ... 'cause I feel I'm a person.

In fact, it is quite common for women to comment that they hate the word.[6] Marion, for example:

hated the word.... That was one of the worst things is thinking that I was a widow.... I still don't like it.

Several of the women maintain that they do not think much about being a widow, and that the term does not really conjure up any image for them. But the way in which they discuss the issue makes one wonder if their apparent indifference is a way of continuing to distance themselves from their identity as a widow. Sarah, for example, in response to my question, assured me that

I don't think of myself as any different.... I remember my mother saying ... after my father died ... "I am a widow." ... And she didn't like the word. Well, I said, "Don't use it, just say you're a single lady."

Martha asserted:

It doesn't bother me because I really am a widow.... And I've never really had anyone say, "This is [my husband's] widow." ... They say, "This is [his] wife." ... That's how they usually put it. And that's great when they do that, I feel good about it.... So, I don't say, I'm [C's] widow, I just say [C's] wife. It doesn't bother me, but I know some people don't like to be called widow. That doesn't bother me.

Although Martha claims she doesn't mind using the word widow to refer to herself, it is clear that it is a word she simply does not use. Similarly, Lynn insists that

It's just a name. It's just a name; it doesn't change anything.... [But] I would hate to say, "This is [Lynn], she's a widow."

Whether or not they accept or reject the appellation of widow for themselves, these women have all entered a new stage of their lives. After living through a difficult and emotional transition, they have to learn to deal with every aspect of their lives in new ways. The next chapters will look at how they learn to work out relationships on these new terms as well as how they learn to take on new responsibilities.

### Notes

1 It is unlikely that Audrey was the only woman who felt some relief when her husband died. However, she also commented that the extra-mural nurses had warned her that she would feel relief and that that reaction was normal and not one she should feel guilty about. I would guess that most women would not want to admit to me or to themselves that they had actually been relieved when their husbands died.

2 See "Identity Foreclosure" (van den Hoonaard 1997) for a discussion of the loss of identity expressed by women who have published accounts of their experience as widows.

3 I came across a similar reaction in published, autobiographical accounts of widowhood. For example, M. T. Dohaney (1989, 5-6) wrote: "As my mother would have said, You had a lovely funeral and I thought it a pity you couldn't have witnessed the packed church.... I started searching the crowd for you the minute I got back to the house.... As time passed and there was still no sign of you, I began to get angry. What was keeping you? How could you expect me to wake you, bury you and be a hostess as well? ... Even as I passed the sand-wiches and replenished the tea, I kept an ear cocked for your footsteps on the back veranda."

4 Identifying moments are "telling moments filled with new self-images.... They are telling because they spark sudden realizations [and] reveal hidden images

of self" (Charmaz 1991, 207). See van den Hoonaard (1997) for widows' vivid descriptions of identifying moments in their autobiographical accounts.

5 Not included in this discussion is the reaction of Mimi, a Native woman. The difference in cultures was obvious in her discussion of what being a widow means for native women: "In our language [widow means] one who doesn't have a husband.... They don't seem to mind because we all had a hard life with our husbands. And I imagine they're just as glad, like I am, you know, that you have your freedom back again." The frankness of Mimi's responses to this and a number of other sensitive questions was unique in this group of women.

6 See "Identity Foreclosure" (van den Hoonaard 1997) for a discussion of younger widows' dislike of the term "widow."

# Part Two

## Experiencing Relationships

# Chapter 3

# They Have Their Own Life: Relationships with Children

*T*his chapter will examine factors that affect how widows feel and talk about their relationship with their children. A comfortable balance characterizes the successful negotiation of these relationships. The behaviour of adult children while their fathers were still living and during the period when they were dying either predisposes their mothers to evaluate their later actions positively or negatively. Women's descriptions of these relationships after their husbands' deaths bring into focus the need for older mothers and adult children to find a balance between the children's concern for their mothers and their ability to recognize that their mothers are capable of making decisions and living alone. In their day-to-day relationships, a balance between privacy and support typifies a comfortable situation.

Relationships with stepchildren provide a special case in which the taken-for-granted link between mothers and children is strained. Some adult children may not see their stepmothers as legitimate parts of the family even after many, many years of marriage. Others may never have developed a good relationship with their father and stepmother since their marriage. This area will become more important in the future with the increase in the proportion of people who experience multiple marriages.[1]

---

Notes to chapter 3 are on p. 62.

## Children's Actions during Their Father's Illness

For those women whose husbands died after a long illness, the actions of their children during the course of that illness have a tremendous impact on their relationship in the long term. Some adult children were "there" for their parents while some were not. This has led to appreciation and increased closeness, or to resentment and continuing alienation.

Lydia, for example, reports that her daughter, who lives in another province, came down to be with her during her husband's last days:

> I was very fortunate, really, because my daughter ... came down. She was here when her father died. Then she had to go back for a week ... but then she came back. Then I went [to her home] for a couple of weeks.

The warmth of Lydia's feelings for her daughter are evident in the way she talks about her.

Perhaps the most significant action taken by an adult child was recounted by Peg. Her husband, who died of cancer, had had the disease previously. Their daughter decided that it was likely that her father would have a recurrence of the cancer, and so she said:

> "I'm going to become a nurse; I'm going to be there for Dad." That's how she became a nurse.

During Peg's husband's final illness, they moved down to their daughter's home in another city where they had "professional [care] right in the house" and Peg could be with him twenty-four hours a day.

Women also have warm remembrances of support they received from their children right after their husband's death. Lynn, for example, reports her sons being "just stupendous" as one of her most vivid memories of the days right after her husband died. Sylvia, whose children live quite far away, returned again and again during the course of our discussion to her son's coming to be with her after her husband's death:

> The real strong one was [my older son]. Our relationship's better, definitely.... I admire him and I appreciate him.... When I needed [him], he was right here.... They drove up almost immediately.

This support is especially significant because Sylvia's husband was her children's stepfather.

Both Sylvia and Peg compare the actions of their other children unfavourably to the children who were there when they were needed. Sylvia describes herself as "sad" that her two other children did not come to her husband's funeral. They "let [her] down." Although Sylvia refers to this as "water under the bridge," it is clear that it has become a continuing emotional obstacle to their relationship.

Peg attributes her son's insufficient presence when his father was ill to the relationship he has with his wife:

> I love him and he loves me, but he has to make sure she is first. An unhappy incident when his father was dying and we called him one evening and said ... "If you want to see Dad, you'd better come down." They had been down a couple of times, but only when it suited her.... "Why, do you think I should?" What are you supposed to say?

Peg commented that her son has to work out these issues with his wife, but it is clear that this has had an important impact on Peg's relationship with both her son and daughter-in-law:

> I love him and he loves me, but he has to make sure that she is first.

She feels that the balance between obligations of a son and obligations of a husband are out of kilter and have led to her son's neglecting his responsibilities towards her in favour of his wife. To this day she finds that if she needs anything, she needs to ask her son, but that her daughter and her husband do not need to be asked—they just do whatever is needed.

June's husband had Alzheimer's disease, and her relationship with her son seems to have been irreparably damaged by the time his father died. June refers back to an episode that occurred eight years before her husband's death. She and her husband had a mobile home in Florida, and her son and his family told them that they were coming to visit:

> And I was so pleased that they were coming to see their father.... I went out and bought a lot of things ... even changed my mobile home.... I got a bigger mobile.... I phoned them and told them there was plenty of room.

This was when the trouble started. June's son had a package deal at a hotel. When she found that they could get their deposit from the hotel back, they responded by saying, "We don't want to impose; you've got enough." June's son and his family had their meals with June, which was "harder ... than to have them sleeping here." In the end, the family left early one evening to go back to the hotel because the children were tired. The next morning June discovered that they had actually gone back to the hotel to go swimming. June's relationship with her son has never been the same:

> They never came to see us as a family again, though my son's a teacher and was free all summer, every summer. They never came again until [my husband] died.

At the funeral, moreover, June's grandsons did not wear what she considered to be the proper attire. That might not have mattered if June had not already been angry about earlier events:

And here were all these lovely children [of friends] with their little blazers on and their shirts and ties, and there were my two grandsons with a pair of jeans and sneakers and not even a jacket on. And I mean *they didn't even know their grandfather* [emphasis added].

At the time of our interview, June summed up her relationship with her son and his family by saying, "I have no attachment to them."

Regardless of how women interpret what their children did or did not do when their husbands were dying, their relationship changes irrevocably after their husbands die. Their adult children may see them as helpless and in need of protection. The next section will look at how women feel about this reaction.

### "I Must Look after Mama"[2]

When they become widows, many women have to renegotiate their relationship with their children. Their children see them as more vulnerable and react by becoming more protective of them. Widows certainly want their children to acknowledge their loss and to be available to support them both emotionally and instrumentally, but when the equilibrium becomes skewed towards overprotectiveness, many women feel besieged in their struggle to build a new life for themselves. Eight women experienced a variety of protective reactions on the part of their children.

Muriel felt that her daughter's inclination to "take over" grew out of a misunderstanding of how her marriage had worked. She said that her daughter had thought that her husband had "been in charge," but that this perception was incorrect. This led to an immediate confrontation:

Especially my daughter, she had this idea that Daddy was gone, "What's going to happen to Mommy? She's going to become a couch potato." I can look after myself. And I said, "[I] have to," to myself, I said "that there's only one person who's going to look after me and it's me."

The initial problem was Muriel's daughter's questioning her capacity to make decisions:

"Oh, Mom, are you sure you can do that? Do you think you can do that? Are you sure you couldn't do that?"

Muriel feels that if she hadn't "displayed some strength" right away, a pattern might have been set up, resulting in her daughter's making all the decisions for her and her becoming dependent on her daughter. Now, not only does she feel that her daughter knows her better than she had before, but she also "grew up quite a bit [and] learned something from that." They have found a way to interact that is comfortable for both of them.

Eileen found that her daughters' attempts to be protective grew out of their concern for her safety. She reported that they

> made me go through a whole bunch of medical tests ... get a new car.... In fact, they wanted me to get a phone in the car.

Her daughters also questioned her ability to make decisions and worried that she would run out of money. Her response was: "When I need money, I'll let you know." Eileen, thus, took a middle road. She complied with some of her children's wishes, but she also made it quite clear to them that "I haven't lost my mind yet; I know what I want and I know what I'm going to do." Like Muriel, Eileen succeeded in training her children to give her the space she needed.

Relationships with sons seem to be more problematic. They, too, are eager to protect their mothers from perceived vulnerability, but sons are not as willing to back off when their mothers try to tell them that they are being too protective. This is exemplified by sons' reactions to their mothers buying a new car. Polly, for example, commented that her sons insisted on coming with her when she was negotiating the price of a used car she was buying from a dealer. She felt that she knew the asking price was fair because she had been looking for a few weeks, but her sons said:

> "No, one of us will go with you." ... M. went with me and he laid out the conditions.

While Judy did not find that her son insisted on being involved in the buying of a new car, his comments suggest a certain level of condescension in referring to her as "the little old lady from Pasadena" when she bought a sports car. This son has also begun to admonish his mother to "be careful driving." Judy refers to this as a "role reversal," which highlights the potential for her to allow her son to make all her important decisions for her. This role reversal is not total, because Judy and other women in this situation may or may not acquiesce to their children's expectations that they become like obedient children.

Edith has experienced the most extreme example of role reversal. As with Judy and Polly, her sons want to take over car maintenance.[3] In addition, her son reacts strongly if Edith says anything that is upsetting:

> He came one lunch time and I was crying and he said, "Mom, you shouldn't be crying.... You should be glad Dad's out of his agony." ... If I say anything to my son that's upsetting to him, he says, "Oh, Mom, you shouldn't be thinking that way."[4]

But, it does not stop there. Edith's sons insist that she let them know where she is when not at home, especially at night:

I mean, now I call them and I say, "If you call the house and I'm not there, I'm at ..." or "I'm here tonight" or something like that.... Goodness, I'm not a child!

Edith fell down her stairs one night, and now she finds that her sons are pressuring her to sell her home and move into a mobile home. Her reaction:

I've lived here thirty-eight years. I fell down the stairs once, now I'm going to move.... "No," I said, "I don't tell you how to live your life ... so you're not going to tell me." Very nasty I thought.

Nonetheless Edith reports that her eldest son "went around to all my sons and said, 'And you keep on at Mom.'" Her feeling is that daughters are easier than sons. She finds that her sons frequently put pressure on her to allow them to make important decisions for her. They certainly do not treat her like the competent adult she feels she is.

It is clear that Edith finds her relationship with her sons almost smothering. Polly, on the other hand, appreciates her son's concern for her welfare. This is illustrated by the difference in the way she relates her experiences:

I often wake up in the middle of the night.... Well, I got up and I put on the light and it wasn't two minutes when the phone rang and it was my daughter-in-law.... "Are you all right?"

The reason Polly's daughter-in-law knew that she had turned on the light is that Polly now lives in an apartment that her son put in over the garage on his property:

Now, my other son ... when we first started talking about building this place, he said, "Mom, I won't rest until you're in town.... Every time I call you and you don't answer, I have you laying at the bottom of those stairs, or falling down with a load of wood in your arms." ... I find that they worry more about me.

But for Polly this has worked out well. She feels that she and her son and daughter-in-law have a good balance between their desire to know that she's safe and their privacy and independence. Polly insists that "my kids don't smoke in my house." As well, she makes an effort to ensure that neither she nor her son's family intrude on one another:

I don't go and sit in their house for hours at a time, and ... I didn't want to [babysit for them].... My attitude is ... I don't want to be part of their rearing.... I see these kids do things that I would never allow my kids to do.... I won't say anything, so I just steer clear.

In contrast, some women report that their children did not take over or try to protect them. Several attribute this reaction to their children's having seen them as quite competent before their husbands died. For example, Emily and her husband had been in business together. Interestingly, the example she chose to explain that her children felt she would be able to make important decisions involved buying a car:

> As far as knowing what to do, like buying my car, my kids feel that I should know ... simply because I worked, I think.

Because she does not feel she has to struggle with her children to retain her independence, Emily

> ask[s] them more advice ... not necessarily that I'm going to do what they tell me, but they know what I'm thinking versus just—I talked about a car a long while before, and they'd say, "Just go get one." ... And if I made a decision to sell the house, I'd talk to them all.

Lydia's responsible position in a large, voluntary organization has shown her children that "I am able to look after myself," while Peg sees her strong personality throughout life as important. For others, it is simply that their children see them as competent adults:

> I'm young and healthy and should be independent.... They feel I'm as busy as I need to be.

Trust is an integral part of this type of relationship. Because their children have not overreacted to their losing their husbands by treating them like children, several women commented that they know that if they do become incompetent in some way as they get older, they can trust their children to tell them when they can no longer function independently:

> But I told [my children] if they think that I get um ... they're worried about me being here, like if I'm starting to leave the stove on or I'm falling down or doing something. I said, "Then you talk me into selling [the house]." (Sarah)

But whether an individual woman is satisfied with the level of concern on the part of her children or not, she does find that the centre of the family has changed:

> It used to be Mom and the kids. Now, it's reversed, the kids and there's Mom. (Blanche)[5]

*Close Feelings*

For the most part, whether their children are protective or not, the widows report that their relationships with their children are close. This became immediately apparent when I asked simply if their relationships with their children had changed since the deaths of their husbands. Martha, for example, reported that her relationship had changed very little:

> We've always been a close family.... We have always been a close family, sort of concerned for each other.

Those who do report a changed relationship most often couch it in the direction of a stronger rather than a more distant relationship. Eileen, for example, said, "I think it's gotten stronger, really." Doris remarked:

> If it has changed, it would be closer because ... they've been very good about being here more because I'm alone.... There's never been any dispute among us or anything, and ... I see more of them, it's a closer relationship.

Audrey felt that her daughter and son-in-law had become

> more considerate.... More concerned about where I am and letting me know where they are.

But simply characterizing relationships as changed or unchanged conceals the complex and subjective nature of women's feelings about their relationships with their children, which are partially grounded in objectively measurable actions but significantly affected by their expectations about what their children should do for and/or with them.

For example, as most researchers have found (e.g., Doyle et al. 1994 and Fengler et al. 1983), most women prefer to live alone rather than with their children. Nonetheless, although the women who participated in this study also preferred living alone, several were quite pleased to report that their children had offered to have them move in with them (Peg, Eleanor, Eileen). Their reasons for declining such an invitation reflect a desire not to threaten a good relationship:

> I definitely think it would be ... disastrous to live with your children. I don't think I'd ever do that. It's been offered to me by my daughter, but I said, "No, I don't think so." (Peg)[6]

Both of Eleanor's daughters-in-law offered to have her come live with them, but she would have had to move a distance to live with either one:

> I'd never be happy in Ontario.... I would have [my son and his family] there.... Granted you make new friends, but I don't want to go up there. I don't want to live free in their basement and the kids would come home

after school and Grandma would be there.... I have a good relationship [with my sons].... I don't ever want to feel that I'm smothering them.

Cathy's experience of moving into the same apartment building as one of her daughters demonstrates that women might be right when they are concerned that living too close to their children could damage their relationship. She has moved away from friends, thus isolating herself, and, although it is more "convenient," she observed that perhaps she's living "a little too close." Cathy's emotional needs require more than her daughter can give, making her feel both neglected and demanding. The hoped-for emotional support has not developed, and Cathy returned again and again during our interview to her disappointment and feeling that she had "expected too much."

Eileen's decisions regarding living arrangements reflect a more conscious exploration of the balance between privacy and independence than those of Cathy, who was responding to persuasion from her daughters. Her initial concerns about leaving her house empty when she travelled led to her idea to build a wing onto the new house her daughter was planning to build. She waited a year after coming to this conclusion before listing her house for sale. Eileen remembered:

> the more I thought about it, the more I thought, "Gee, that's a good idea," 'cause I could be close to [my daughter and her family] and at the same time I could have my independence. I wanted my own garage and I said ... "I could build that wing onto your house." They agreed and the plans are being drawn up.[7]

This move was instigated by Eileen, and her focus on her own privacy and independence reflects an approach that adds the needed balance to her relationship with her daughter.

Simply acknowledging a particularly difficult time is also very meaningful. One of Eleanor's sons remembered to call her on the anniversary of her husband's death as well as on Father's Day, because he knew that those days would be very emotional for her. Audrey's one daughter, who lives in Australia, "sent flowers on the anniversary of [my husband's] death." It may be that the geographic distance allows these adult children to show their concern without their feeling a risk of being overwhelmed.

Neglecting to notice an important date can be very hurtful. Cathy was not only disappointed but hurt by her daughters' not understanding how meaningful her fiftieth wedding anniversary was to her:

> This was our fiftieth anniversary.... And that kind of provoked me ... 'cause I was talking to [one of] the girls [her daughters] ... and I said, "This is our

anniversary." She said, "Yes, I know, Mom." ... I let it go at that.... I was talking to the other girl here so she said, "You sound kind of down today." ... Well, I said, "I am a little bit.... This is our anniversary day." "I know," she said, "but Dad's dead," she said, "Dad's gone." So I said, "Dad's gone, but I'm still here." It really hurt me, really hurt me.

Cathy and her daughters have not found a balance between what she needs to assuage her loneliness and what they feel is reasonable. This may be one reason why they tried to underplay the importance of Cathy's fiftieth wedding anniversary. Cathy reports that members of a support group she attends had predicted that her daughters would "have you over for supper ... or something for your anniversary."

Weekends are particularly difficult times for widows, and Eileen, Doris and Lynn reported that they often spend their weekends with their children. Eileen noted:

Weekends I go with the kids.... I go to [their house] and spend it with [them].... That has helped me get through the weekends.

Doris found that

Weekends were bad and weekends are still bad if I'm alone, but I'm most fortunate in that I'm not as a rule alone because the one son isn't married, and there's been very few weekends since his father died that he hasn't come either Saturday or Sunday and spent the better part of a day.... My daughter comes most weekends, every other weekend or so.

Audrey's daughter knows that her mother finds hearing particular hymns difficult and puts her arm around her mother when they are sung at church, while Sarah's daughter knows that one of the things she misses most is having tea with her husband when returning from an evening outing:

Now the kids always come in with me and say, why even if it's eleven o'clock and [my daughter] has so far to go, she says, "Oh, I think I'll have a cup of tea before I go," or something like that. I know why they're doing it.... They always do that; they always come in.

For women who live quite close to their children it is the day-to-day thoughtfulness that defines their relationship with those children. Martha has one daughter who "hardly misses a day she doesn't call me since her father died." Her other two daughters are not as conscientious, but they do give her the feeling that they appreciate her calling them:

The second one is terrible.... I call her ... she is very busy.... She just doesn't have the time, so I'll call her and I'll say, "Oh, you're alive. I just called to make sure you're still there." She says, "Well, Mom, I'm so glad you called because ... I do neglect." But I don't let it bother me because I know she's busy.

Martha's third daughter lives "right up the road" from her and also depends on her mother to keep in touch:

> She said, "Come in, drop in anytime," she said, "at all." 'Cause, she said, "I know I don't visit you as often as I should ... but you know I'm here."

Martha's explanation is that the two inattentive daughters have very busy lives. Therefore, it is only reasonable that she takes responsibility for initiating their contacts. This is compensated for by their not feeling that Martha is intruding or asking too much by calling or visiting them when she feels like it.

Sarah believes she is always in her children's thoughts, and described regular contact that reflected this feeling:

> My daughter calls me every night before she goes to bed.... She usually calls me every morning before she goes to work.... My daughter-in-law calls me if she hasn't heard from me or one of the kids.

Florence also related the daily concern of her son and his family:

> They always check on me every day.... There's never a day goes by that there's a.... [My son] most generally comes in every night on his way home ... and if [my daughter-in-law] phones up and I'm out in the shed or something and don't answer the phone, she'll try twice and if I don't answer it, then she'll be right up to make sure I'm all right.... At least once a day, somebody's going to check ... a good feeling to know they'll do that.

The balance between this feeling of appropriate caring and overprotection makes the difference between a mother's being satisfied or dissatisfied with her relationship with her adult children.

Several women talk about their relationships with their children in ways that make it clear that they maintain balance by adding reciprocity to the relationship. For example, Eileen babysits for her grandchildren when her daughter travels, and her daughter includes her in many family outings. Judy and her sons joke that she will make her special goulash and that they will come visit her with their friends. Florence's son invites her for dinner regularly, and she, in turn, will often cook food in quantity and invite him and his family to join her.

Sarah's discussion of her relationship with her children reflects a very refined system of maintaining reciprocity and balance in their relationship. The foundation is a broad understanding of their not intruding on one another:

> And my family, well, they're just wonderful; they're friends as well as family. If I need anything, I only have to make a phone call. And if I don't want them around, they don't crowd me.

In exchange, Sarah handles her difficult times by herself:

> I don't feel sorry for myself.... I give myself a bawling out. I just sit down and say, "Now look, this is the way things are." And it helps.

Sarah recounted a number of arrangements that rest on the firm foundation of reciprocity she has established with her children. They asked her not to learn to drive because they felt they would worry about her, "Mom, we've got enough worries with you living alone." In return, "We'll take you any place you want to go." Sarah feels very comfortable calling on her children if there is something she cannot fix, but she usually tries to fix things herself before calling on them. She enjoyed explaining that after she had spent over an hour putting up one of a set of new venetian blinds, her son came over to help. She went into another room for just a few minutes, and when she returned, he said:

> "Your blind's up." He said, "I could have done that the first time, but I knew you wanted to do it." So he let me try it.

Sarah spends her winters in Florida, which means that she needs someone to pay her local bills for her and to keep an eye on her house. Sarah's daughter pays the bills for her, and her son checks on her house for her. The reciprocity involved is very ingenious:

> Yeah, well my son is very fond of ice cream, and he can't get cable [TV] ... and he loves TV. So I fill the freezer downstairs with ice cream, and I know he'll be down to watch TV. And he watches the house.... He checks to make sure that everything's all right.

In addition, Sarah's granddaughter, who attends university, "if she wants to entertain, she brings the kids down, cooks them supper." For Sarah, there is the tremendous benefit of having family members check her house in an unpredictable but reliable fashion:

> So there's always some, they never know.... They never know whether I'm here or not.

Not everyone is successful at maintaining or implementing a more reciprocal relationship. For example, Sylvia has tried to persuade her children to visit her by offering them "whatever they want" of some of the nice things her husband left her. This has not been effective, and she fears she will soon have to call an antique dealer. Edith, whose sons have become so domineering, has tried to insert an element of reciprocity by inviting them to have some holiday meals at her home, but they insist she come to theirs, thus reinforcing the unequal dimension that has become a part of their relationship. Cathy, who is so aware that she is overwhelming her daughters who live in the same town with her need for their support, talked of moving to another town where she has a daughter who does not have a job. Her hope is that they would be company for one another.

A change in the circumstances of the mother or adult child can also upset the equilibrium they have achieved. In June's case, this occurred when her daughter, who was divorced, became involved in a serious relationship that included her sharing a residence with her partner. Not only does June's daughter not have as much time to spend with her, but

> It doesn't seem the same because he's built this house. [My daughter] had a house.... I felt it was her house, and I could go in any time. But it's different now.... I feel I've got to call and make sure.

June remarked, "I'm glad she's happy, but I still miss her because I don't feel I can just drop in and do things with her."

For Eleanor, the change in equilibrium was brought about by her becoming involved in a relationship with a man. This has upset her son, who was particularly bothered when she removed her wedding rings. She commented that it left her wondering why she felt she had to make excuses to her son. Her conclusion: "The roles do reverse."

For women, who do not live near their children, the telephone can be a lifeline that results in a long-distance relationship's being as close or closer emotionally than a relationship with a child living in the same town or neighbourhood. Lydia, for example, has a closer relationship with her daughter who lives out of the province than she does with the one who lives a fifteen-minute drive away:

> [My daughter in Quebec] keeps in touch.... She usually calls every two weeks, she keeps in touch.... She and I get along really well. But my daughter [who lives in the next town] is a little more.... I don't seem to be able to reach her as easily.... I think she has so much she tries to keep from me like this [kidney disease]. She doesn't want me to worry about her.... We go out to lunch once in a while.

Unfortunately, long-distance phone calling can be very expensive, and this affects Sylvia, whose children all live in the United States:

> I'm a demon on the phone. I call home too many times, and I've just got to....
> I talked to my daughter last night.... I just had something to tell her ... and I've just got to learn to be, that's so expensive, on a smaller budget, you see.

For Sylvia, finding the balance between finances and loneliness is not an easy task.

The women's expectations of their children and other relatives also coloured their feelings about their relationships. Children and other family members did not always live up to widows' expectations. This occurred either in the performing of tasks or in failing to provide emotional support. Frances at eighty-seven depended on relatives to do much of her shopping for her because she didn't drive. She expressed frustration and hurt at her niece who had "backed off a little bit" and wondered if she "expect[ed] too much."

Cathy, who had moved to her daughter's apartment building at that daughter's urging, had expected this daughter to provide considerable emotional support. But this daughter seemed not to have much patience for Cathy's expressions of loneliness, and Cathy found it very difficult to make friends in her new building because it was not a place where one ran into people. Her expected support was not forthcoming; she was very disappointed and pondered whether or not she had expected too much. This was particularly poignant on what would have been her fiftieth wedding anniversary.

June's expectations of social support were initially satisfied. She and her daughter had spent a great deal of time together in the days after June's husband died. Her daughter recently became involved in a romantic relationship and, as a result, is less available. This left her mother expecting to see her much more than she did. June felt deserted and forgotten.

These women, who had expected more support from their family members than they got, voiced great disappointment and sometimes resentment. Others, who received less support from their children also expected less—they were not disappointed and felt that things were proceeding as they should. Blanche, for example, commented that her children "are very good; they come when they can," which was not very often.

### Stepchildren as a Special Case

With the rising divorce rate, more and more women are involved with children their husbands had from a previous marriage, a combination of their husband's and their own children from a previous marriage and, as with Sylvia (discussed in an earlier section), children of their own from a previous marriage. This is a complex area we know little about, but five of the twenty-seven participants in this study were married to men who had had children from a previous marriage. The stories they tell about relationships with those children paint a complex picture. Some had a fairly distant relationship with these children during the life of the marriage. Others describe relationships that brought disappointments in the wake of their husbands' deaths. Only one of the five talks of a continuing close relationship.

Marilyn provides an example of a widow whose stepchildren had resented her marriage to their father. As a result, she had never been close to them. Nonetheless, it was difficult for Marilyn that her husband's sons were "not kind to him during his final days.... They just didn't go see him." His daughters, on the other hand, were always "civil" and one did see her father regularly during his illness. Nonetheless, when Marilyn had her husband cremated, as he had requested, his children were upset because "they said I had denied them their final farewell." She felt that she had simply followed her husband's wishes and that his children had had time to say good-bye while he was still alive. Therefore, even though Marilyn had never had a close relationship with her husband's children, she still felt angry with them on his behalf. Had they been more considerate to their father when he was alive, Marilyn might have responded by taking their wishes into account after his death.

Marion, on the other hand, has found that her relationship with her husband's daughter improved in the years before his death and continued afterwards. Marion was many years younger than her husband and is only one year older than his daughter. In recent years they have become "very close friends." There is a contrast between her reaction and that of Marilyn. While Marilyn felt that her stepchildren had relinquished the right to have an opinion about funeral arrangements, Marion has been waiting to make a decision about her husband's ashes until she can find something "acceptable to his daughter, who is religious." Consequently, Marion and her stepdaughter are continuing a mutually satisfying relationship while Marilyn and her stepchildren have almost no relationship at all.

To some extent, Betty's and Judy's relationships with their husbands' children have been complicated by problems over material possessions and who has the legitimate right to make decisions regarding those possessions. Betty and her husband had one son, and her husband, a widower, brought two grown sons to their marriage, which lasted forty-six years. The relationships were complex even before Betty's husband died because there had always been "some jealousy between my son and my stepsons because they both vie to be the tops." After her husband died, Betty's children seemed to get along better than they had for awhile, but that did not last long. According to Betty's son, "We just don't hit it off." At least some of the tension between the half-brothers appears to be based on different levels of material success. Indeed, Betty finds that her stepsons even are envious of the amount of money her husband left to her.

But the more serious issue for Betty surrounds a large CD collection of classical music, which her husband had accumulated over his lifetime. Betty had felt that her children were not interested in this collection or in the histories that her husband had compiled about them. Consequently, some time after her husband had died, Betty gave the collection to a person who, she felt, would really enjoy and appreciate it. This caused unforeseen problems for, although Betty and her husband had been married for many years, his sons still felt that she did not have the right to decide the fate of what they considered to be a family possession:

> Look, [my son] wouldn't know one end of an overture from the other. Neither did [my stepson]. But all of the sudden he wanted it, and I had given it away.... He sent one of his girls after it and said it belongs in the family. And I didn't know 'til he got it back, what had happened, and that has made much trouble. Because he shouldn't have done that. It was mine; it was not his to do with and it made me ... the stepmother.... He just figured it should go in the family.

For Betty, this is the most significant of a "lot of little things" that have made her relationship with her stepsons "unpleasant."

Judy, whose marriage was much shorter—ten years—had a run-in with her stepchildren based on their concern that she not abscond with too much of their father's estate. She communicates a sense of shock regarding the actions of stepchildren who "changed right before my eyes." This occurred in conjunction with the reading of her husband's will:

> When I was reading the will ... I was going slowly and asking if there was anything they wanted me to read over.... I read where it said his RRIF.[8] ... I heard, "Yeah, she got the money."

This comment was followed by Judy's stepchildren coming by to go through their father's things to make sure they got what was listed in his will. When Judy was moving out of her husband's house, which he had left to his children by mutual agreement with Judy, they showed up again to "see that I didn't take anything" that they considered theirs. Judy says she was "devastated" by what had happened.[9] She has very little contact with her stepchildren now and expresses particularly a longing for her husband's grandchildren. She remarks:

> I really did expect them to keep in touch with me. They didn't; they haven't said "boo."

Polly was the only one of these five women who describes a relationship with stepchildren that has been close over the long term. In fact, she recounts an incident that illustrates her stepsons' strong desire to maintain their relationship after their father's death:

> And the oldest one, I stopped to see him ... and he hugged me and said, "I want to ask you something.... Am I still number-one son?" ... I said, "Of

course, why would that change?" And his eyes all filled with tears and he said, "I was just afraid that it might ... after Daddy was gone."

Polly takes great pride in the success she and her husband had in blending their two families during their twenty-seven years of marriage. She told me that her daughter boasts about having six brothers. She said:

> I never allowed [my husband] to make any distinctions. When we put the families together, we had seven kids.

Polly had the advantage of marrying her husband when their children were still children, and this has had a positive effect: "No, I never had any trouble with the kids at all."

## Conclusion

The material in this chapter reinforces the mixed findings of other research about whether relationships with adult children benefit older widows (O'Bryant and Hansson 1995). This is not surprising, because intergenerational relationships are complex and are affected by patterns and feelings established prior to the widow's husband's death (Mancini and Blieszner 1989) as well as by how adult children act after their fathers die.

Implicit in the comments of most of these women is a sense that, although most expect their children to be aware of and sensitive to their needs, these adult children have their own lives to live and their mothers need to be sure not to overstep an invisible boundary that would result in invading privacy, crowding or expecting too much. As well, adult children can overstep the boundary that makes the difference between their treating their mother like a competent adult for whom they care a great deal, either attempting to force her into the role of the obedient child or conversely causing her to feel abandoned.

Thus, we see a balancing act that goes on between an older widow and her children. There is also an indication that mothers are aware that their children are trying to balance their relationship with their own spouses and their relationship with their widowed mother, as is the case with Peg's son. This may be a more important issue for sons, and several women commented that daughters feel a stronger tie to their mother than sons do.

Sarah Matthews (1979), in her important study *The Social World of Old Women*, conceptualized this balancing act as old mothers' attempts to redress the imbalance of power that exists between them and their adult children. The women in this study also seek a balance, but they see the issue as one of finding a level where each person feels she or he is contributing equally to the relationship. They, like the women in Matthews's book, are very sensitive to the feeling that their children have their own lives to live.

Relationships with children are only one type of a number that are thrown into disarray by the death of one's husband. The negotiation required to establish comfortable and balanced relationships is subtle and complex. Similarly, widows need to renegotiate their ways of interacting with friends and with men. This will be the subject of the next two chapters.

### Notes

1 In 1991, only 4 percent of those over sixty-five reported having divorced at some time in their lives, although the proportion is growing (Novak 1997).

2 According to Eleanor, this was one of her son's reactions to her becoming a widow.

3 See chapter 6 for a more extensive discussion about the relationship of widows to cars and car maintenance, which illustrates the fact that cars are one of the last areas that are still almost totally in the province of men.

4 Sometimes Edith does seem to be using emotional blackmail. She reports commenting: "I say sometimes I feel nobody cares whether I'm here or not. I know they're busy...." So, although some of her sons' reactions are clearly protective, this is not always the reason for their being upset at what she says.

5 Dr. Joyce Brothers, in *Widowed* (1990), her account of her experience with becoming a widow, notes that her children became the centre of the family after her husband's death.

6 It's interesting to note that Peg's father had lived with her for about the last ten years of his life, and she said that this had been a good arrangement. Nonetheless, she strongly felt that living with either of her children might jeopardize their relationship.

7 In a recent conversation, Eileen told me that she has, indeed, moved into a wing that she built onto her daughter's house and that things are working out very well.

8 Registered Retirement Income Fund.

9 This has obviously had a profound effect on Judy. She started off our interview talking about the betrayal of her stepchildren and brought it up many times during the interview.

# Chapter 4

# Relationships with Friends

$T$his chapter will explore what widows say about their relationships with their friends. It will first address the obligations women felt they had towards their friends, the foremost being "keeping up appearances" and not seeming too depressed. It will then examine the ambiguity surrounding what widows can reasonably expect their friends to do for them. Finally, the chapter will explore the concept of a "couples' world" that widows used to explain the social context in which they find themselves.

There were certain approaches the widows needed to take to maintain relationships with their friends, or even to make new friends. The first was "to keep up appearances," i.e., to be fairly cheerful and upbeat. Second, some indicated that *they* took the initiative to keep in touch with friends while others felt that their friends should have made the effort to include them in social activities. Their expectations about these responsibilities had an impact on whether their friendships continued or not and on how they interpreted what had happened.

### Keeping Up Appearances

Most women averred that it was important to "keep up appearances" when they are around other people. They felt they should not cry, be very down or talk about their husbands too much in front of others. Several commented

---

Notes to chapter 4 are on p. 75.

that if you need to cry, you should cry alone. It was not their friends' responsibility to cope with the loss of their husband, but theirs (often alone). If you cried in front of your friends or appeared too depressed you would:

depress your friends;

bore everybody;

drive people crazy; or

burden people.

Others wouldn't understand and would "get fed up" with a widow who was always sad. One woman even informed me that

if I'd have wept and wailed and howled in [my friends'] soup for the last six months ... [my husband] would be very upset with me ... very disapproving ... ashamed of me. (Lynn)

A few women did not have much patience for widows who could not control their emotions in public. They were as unsympathetic towards those who broke the feeling rules as those who had not experienced widowhood themselves. Feeling rules are the guidelines that direct "how we want to try to feel" (Hochschild 1979, 563). We know if we are conforming to or breaking feeling rules by others' reactions to the emotions we project. There were a number of stories about widowed friends who were too depressing to be with. One woman even avoided her own sister because she was crying all the time. This inclination to keep away from depressing widows was reinforced by others. For example:

I had a friend ... acquaintance, and she lost her husband shortly after [me] ... so I was trying to be of comfort to her and ... it drug me down ... and my daughter-in-law took me aside.... And she says, "Emily, you can't take that, you know ... you need to be around people that are uplifting."[1]

Nonetheless, a few widows did identify settings in which they were able to share their grief with a group or an individual who understood what they were going through. Some attended a support group for widows and commented that talking about their feelings was both expected and helpful (see chapter 8 for a discussion of support groups). Others identified a particular friend, who was also widowed, with whom they "could talk and share ... similar experiences" (Audrey).

Reciprocity is the necessary ingredient for one's being able to let go and talk about what it really feels like to lose a husband.[2] The women who lost patience with other widows who talked about their loss all the time felt burdened by unwanted confidences. All the women knew that their married friends would not understand how they felt. Marie reported that a widow who lived down the street from her had called and offered to listen if she needed to talk. But Marie felt that

> She was a nice woman, I liked her, but I mean, no, no. No, I don't know her.

She felt neither the inclination to talk nor to listen to her neighbour talk about the feelings surrounding the loss of her husband.

Confining their emotions to the proper context required great control. As Doris commented:

> Well, you're going to go away from here thinking that I'm fine and I feel fine. Maybe you won't be at the end of the road 'til I'll be weeping, but that's all right.

For some women, being in control even when alone demonstrated that they were not *stuck* and could go on with life. There was a great deal of emotion work involved in these women's interpretation of how they felt around others and how they felt around themselves. Emotion work requires one to try to have feelings that are appropriate for a particular situation (Hochschild, 1979), and what was appropriate for most of these widows was being able to move from feelings of overwhelming grief and sadness to feelings that they could manage and go on with life. This was particularly evident among those of British origin, whose comments evoked impressions of Londoners' stiff upper lip during the Blitz. Several commented that they had to take themselves in tow and simply make themselves feel better. Lydia said:

> I just decided I have to pull myself together, you know, take the bull by the horns. I have always tried to be very cheerful about the whole thing.

She has worked on her emotions sufficiently that she even interprets her grandchildren's experience of witnessing their grandfather's illness as worse than her own experience of losing a husband.

Other women explained that their husbands would want them to get on with their lives and not spend all their time crying. In this way they were able to fulfil societal expectations at the same time that they were pleasing their husbands.

A few women commented that they did not want to upset their adult children by letting them see the extent of their suffering. Sarah, for example, explained that

> Oh, there's days you get down a little bit, but you, I talk to myself or go and do a craft ... so I talk to myself and think, "You're darn fortunate." Or I think of someone who's sick

rather than lean on her children when she had an "upset moment." There were two notable exceptions.

As mentioned in the previous chapter, Cathy has moved to a new apartment to live in the same building as her daughter. She still finds that she could not "seem to get myself up." She has been unable to perform the expected emotion work and her daughters, especially the one who lives in her building, become "cross" and "resent" the sympathy Cathy feels she should get from her children. She was in the uncomfortable position of feeling that her daughters should be more understanding at the same time that she believed she was asking too much of them. It was clear from the way Cathy told her story that she felt that she ought to have been more successful at controlling how she felt, that she should have been more effective in her emotion work.

Audrey, on the other hand, initially thought that her daughter and son-in-law were not very understanding. She had been trying to protect them from the strength of her feelings of loss. Finally, on a bad day, "it all came out." When this happened, she discovered that they had not realized what she "was going through." After that Audrey found them to be much more considerate. This included more invitations to dinner as well as her daughter's becoming more loving. Audrey's lapse at control had very positive results. She commented:

> I guess I should have done it sooner. I was trying to be strong and put up a good front, you know.

Conforming to feeling rules may, in most cases, mean that one does not drive others away, but in this case it had got in the way of Audrey's relationship with her children.

Although there are rules regarding the display and even the feeling of emotions in response to the loss of one's spouse, it is less clear what widows have the right to expect from their friends and what their own obligations are in order for friendships, in particular, to be maintained.

### Expectations

Because there do not seem to be any generally accepted norms for interaction, women's interpretation of what has gone on is very much affected by what *they* had assumed was their right to expect from their friends, acquaintances and children. These expectations had a great influence over their explanation of how their relationships had changed.

When a woman becomes widowed, she is "dropped" by at least some of her friends (see, e.g., Lopata 1996; van den Hoonaard 1994). This had been common knowledge among many women even before they experienced it. Nonetheless, some were still surprised that it could happen to them:

> You think you're going to be different. (Audrey)

Helena Lopata (1996, 160-61) has suggested a variety of explanations that may help us understand why friends seem to desert widows and why they are so surprised. One possibility is that this surprise may be a result of a confusion between "friendly relations," which carry minimal obligations, and "friendship," which does imply more extensive obligations. This is undoubtedly true in some cases; however, in other cases the picture is more complex. Some women recount the loss of friendships that were many years old, that had included much reciprocal assistance and sharing of confidences (MacRae 1996, 386).

Eileen, for example, recounted the demise of her friendship with a woman she had considered a very good friend. Eileen explained that not only had she known this friend for years, but, when the friend had been seriously ill, Eileen had

> [been] there when she came back from the hospital [and] spent months going to her house, helping her out.

Eileen had thought they were very close friends. After her husband died she visited her friend several times and then she

> called her and I went to her house.... I went to visit her ... and she was very pleased and wanted to see me ... and I said to her, "I was here three weeks ago" ... and I said to her, "This is the last time I'm coming, the last time I'm calling you. Now the ball's in your park. Now, if you don't call me, that means our friendship is finished."

And it was. Eileen felt that she had given her friend every opportunity to continue the relationship.

In contrast, Eileen has acquaintances who have become good friends since her husband's death, some of whom worked with her husband. She noted that they

> called me and invited me to the house for supper or lunch [and] have always called me.... It's been different now, [those I] ... expected to be here all the time, to be friends with, to call you haven't, and others ... that you didn't expect [to call or visit] are the ones that really come forward.

Lopata (1996, 159-60) raises a number of other possibilities that contribute to our thinking about why friends so often desert women who have become widows. First of all, many people "avoid all connections with death," and, therefore, shun all people who have been closely touched by it, as widows and those who are seriously ill have. As well, some people find interaction with widows so "awkward" that they limit contact with them, particularly if they were used to seeing the widow as one half of a couple. Widows' emotions may be so close to the surface that it makes their former friends uncomfortable, and, finally, the "norms of symmetry and sharing" may no longer fit. After all, equality is one of the hallmarks of friendship, and widows have a lower status than do wives.

Of course, a major problem with trying to understand what went wrong in these situations is that researchers generally interview widows but not the friends they feel have deserted them. We are, therefore, left trying to guess what has really happened. However, when I studied life in a Florida retirement community (van den Hoonaard 1992), I did have the opportunity to ask married women if they had any good friends who had become widows in order to find out how they interpreted this phenomenon. Most claimed that they had had no good friends become a widow—hardly credible in a community in which the percentage of households with a single person living in it had gone from 9 percent to 26 percent over a period of ten years. Surely someone had been a friend of one of the women who had lost their husbands. More likely, some women handled their inability to provide support to widowed friends by redefining their relationship from that of friendship to that of friendly relations or acquaintanceship. This result of cognitive dissonance (Festinger 1962) would explain how women living in a *world of widows* could maintain that none of them had previously been good friends.

Older widows' interpretations of the nature of these lost relationships may not be the problem. Rather, it may be that their expectations of how their friends should provide support have affected their understandings of what had gone on. Many expected their friends to call, invite, include or drive them to events. Thus, although Emily's friends from a social organization invited her to a social evening being held by the organization, the difficulty for her was that she felt that they should have offered to drive her there (even though she would still have preferred to take her car). Because they did not offer to drive her, she did not go and felt excluded.

Peg, on the other hand, felt that it was *her* responsibility to keep in touch with her friends:

> You just have to make the effort of keeping going with people.... I network; I keep it going.... I'm not going to drift into the woodwork, vanish into the wallpaper.

She described a number of occasions when she had invited people to her home and had made conscious efforts to stay in touch with others. It did not seem to trouble her that she had to make the effort. In fact, this was simply the way she expected things to be.

Lynn also saw keeping friendships going as primarily her responsibility. She expected to get fewer invitations, but commented that she was determined to have luncheon parties and dinner parties.... I'm going to make them come ... because that's the only way I'm going to keep in contact with these people.... I can't expect to get invited out if I don't receive.

Contrast this approach to Eileen's, who noted: "I've given [my friend] the chance." Others who felt neglected conceded that they had not called their friends who had "disappeared." Perhaps, as single women, they, like some widows in Florida (van den Hoonaard 1994), did not feel that they were in the position to proffer an invitation. Being widowed confers a lowered status (Lopata 1976), and may, therefore, upset the equality that is a hallmark of friendship (Allan 1979; Lopata 1975; Suttles 1970), as well as shift obligations onto one member of the relationship to take the initiative to keep it going. Because the role of "friend" is not institutionalized, norms are often unclear as well as idiosyncratic (Matthews 1986, 58). It appears that, in some cases, both the widow and her friends each assumed the other now has that obligation, and this led to the termination of the friendship.

Concentrating on disappointments, however, presents only part of the picture. Women also have the experience of receiving unexpected support and help. Many women found that there were people who "came through" for them in ways they did not expect. For example, it was not uncommon for neighbours, particularly younger neighbours, to provide instrumental support. Sylvia's neighbours were a young couple who

> did things for me in the house ... checked on and washed out the refrigerator ... helped to do the windows.

Emily found that a few younger business acquaintances "rolled up hoses and did stuff like that."

As well, there were people who provided unexpected emotional support:

> People that were acquaintances have become good friends. (Eileen)

Marie, a nurse, found unexpected support from people she worked with: "I did not think they cared that much." This support took the form of offering a cup of tea or asking how she was doing. Even a small gesture from an unexpected source sometimes made a real difference:

> the girl at the checkout at [the grocery store] ... brought a little bunch of flowers. (Marilyn)

Single women were most likely to go on to become close friends, sometimes unexpectedly. Lydia was surprised that there were so many "people around to do things with ... they are looking for friendship." Others reported picking up friendships with women who were already widows. Edith found that losing her husband made me more aware of other people.... You get in a rut when you're married ... and it doesn't make you care really about other people.

She was disappointed with her married friends who had not called, but was able to see that that had been her own reaction before her husband died.

Regardless of the expectations they had had, these widows felt that the root of the problem was that they were no longer part of a couple. This made interacting much more difficult and made them feel like outsiders. The next section will explore the way in which these widows expressed their position in a couples' world.

### *A Couples' World*

Widows used the term "couples' world" to communicate their feeling of not fitting into society in a comfortable way.[3] They became the "other" in a world that was designed for couples. Their identity was affected, as well as the way they interacted with others. As Helena Lopata notes (1996, 158): "entrance into the role of wife requires a reconstruction of reality." The new reality involves becoming one half of a couple rather than a totally separate individual. McCall and Simmons (1966) recognized that friends may see couples not as two individuals but as a collective unit. Women, particularly older women, often see themselves and their husbands as a collective unit, even today. Entrance into the role of widow or single woman also requires a reconstruction of reality, one that is unwanted and demands much effort.

As a result, when widowed, women felt like they were "half a person" (Sarah). This contributed to a feeling of emptiness, that "something [wa]s missing" (Eileen). Peg felt that she "stuck out like a sore thumb ... where being a couple before was effortless." For some, this made it very difficult to go places where they were known as a couple, for example, church or clubs. Indeed, Doris went to the extent of stating to me that she was not "the same person any more, not a couple."

Special circumstances dictated an even closer feeling of identity. Eleanor, for example, had been married to an amputee. She, therefore, not only felt like half of a couple unit, but pointed out that

I was his leg. I was that missing leg ... and we were really close.

Women who had been in business with their husbands had an identity that was more intertwined with their life as a couple.

Experiences in public places reinforced the feeling that the unit of identity was that of a couple. For example, Emily and her husband had earned a trip to a resort through their business. After he died, Emily decided to go on the trip alone. She found that everything at the hotel was set up under the assumption that everyone there was part of a couple. Consequently, when she asked for a towel for the beach, the attendant gave her two. When she told him that she only wanted one, he responded that

"This is a couples' club" and wanted to know what I was doing there.

This reaction made her feel strange and out of place. She learned to take the two towels without comment rather than to create the upsetting situation of having to explain how a single person had ended up on the tour.

Emily also pointed out that many restaurants and donut shops are eliminating counters. She used to go to a donut shop on the weekend if she just felt the need for company. She could sit at the counter and strike up a conversation with anyone else who happened to be there. The counter provided the perfect opportunity for sociability at any time, night or day. Many shops have taken out their counters and replaced them with tables "so that is sort of taboo." One may sit at a table alone, but the likelihood of engaging in interaction is small.

In fact, going out to a restaurant alone is not an option many women will consider. Some women simply do not entertain the possibility: "Oh, no, not on my own" (Sarah). When the topic of restaurants came up in the "Striving on Your Own" workshop, the participants made the following comments:

You go to restaurants alone? Just to go out? I would never consider going alone.

[If you have to go to a restaurant alone], you eat as quickly as you can and get out. (Field notes)

Other women in the group commented that they never go alone or will go alone, but not at peak times. One woman mentioned that she and her husband used to stop at a lovely inn when they passed a particular town. Now, when she goes past that town, she stays in her car and turns on the CD player and eats a sandwich and has juice. She describes this experience as "a lovely time," which has allowed her to be able to drive past this town without getting upset.

For most of us, going out to a restaurant may conjure up pleasant thoughts of relaxation and sociability, but the women painted a picture that is in stark contrast to this. For example, Blanche describes going to restaurants in less than comfortable terms:

I don't really like going alone, but I will.... No, you sort of sit and stare at your food and gaze into space, listen to what other people are saying at the next table, that sort of thing.

Some women, like Florence, may have "a dish of soup or something" in the shopping mall if they are there, but will not go to a restaurant by themselves. Others will not even eat alone in a food court. When I asked Nancy if she felt comfortable eating alone in a restaurant, she replied:

> No. I'm not. In fact I will come home. I've found that I came home from the mall and I wasn't through shopping because I didn't want to sit down [in the food court] and eat alone. No, that's one time I don't enjoy very much.

Audrey noted that, in general, it's easier to do things when there are two of you, and that some things she simply feels she can't do now that she is alone. For example, she feels constrained from going to a Happy Hour at a local pub on Friday nights, as she used to do with her husband. She tried going with another widow, but

> We'd go maybe ... and then we'd say, "Aren't we stupid, two old fools sitting here." 'Cause you just ... stick out like a sore thumb, and then you'd see all these other women coming and you'd think, "Yeah, there they are out, too." ... [You] just feel like you're there looking for a pickup.... We didn't want to be looked at that way so that didn't just last too long.

In rural areas, church suppers often provide the relaxation and sociability we often associate with going to a restaurant for a meal. But, unless you are easily included with the couples, they make you feel just as alone as going to a restaurant:

> And they have a lot of suppers out here ... around the different churches and things. I won't go to one of them 'cause [my husband] and I used to go to them around Rivertown and places.... I feel so lonesome when I go to any of them that I just won't go at all. I'd sooner stay home than I would to go and ... just be by yourself and eat.... There's nobody to talk to because you go to them and most generally they're couples. And there's nobody to talk to ... there's no sociability [to] it.... And this is what hurts is when I go out amongst people and nobody talks to me. (Florence)

Although Sarah would not consider going to a restaurant by herself, when she is in Florida for part of the year, she does go out to restaurants in groups. She noted that the hardest thing about that situation was realizing that she had to pay for herself:

> I thought, "Oh, I have to pay for this." And little things like that, that you don't think about crop up.

The couple identity had been an effortless one; it just seemed natural and easy. Learning to interact and be a woman alone required more conscious effort for the widow herself and for others who interacted with her.

First, she had to simply make the effort to "seek out others" (Peg), particularly other widows.

Another area of effort was being a host. While married, having a dinner party felt natural to a woman. The tasks of greeting the guests, mixing the drinks, carving the turkey or roast were simply a matter of habit. Each knew his or her role. After her husband had died, a woman had to make an effort to invite people (Audrey). Unable to reproduce the old pattern she felt strange because

> There's things, I mean dumb things you can work around, but they're still there. Like you don't know how to carve ... there are lots of things. (Marion)

Although all these obstacles are solvable, the main result is that dinner parties required more effort than previously, and effort of a new kind. As Marion remarked: "It just isn't the same."

And who sits at the head of the table? Again this was not a major dilemma; the solution might be fairly simple—Lynn avoids facing the empty space by having buffets. Nonetheless, it is one more contribution to the unnatural feeling surrounding once-comfortable situations.

Some widows also noticed that their new status required more effort on the part of their friends. This was most noticeable when they were out as part of a group in which they were the only widow. The effort, not surprisingly, is part of what makes the situation uncomfortable:

> Everybody tries to make it pleasant, but it's not the same. (Eileen)

> They went out of their way to make me feel comfortable. (Eleanor)

The manner of being included underscores an important change in the relationship. Women talked about being included in ways that evoked that sense of otherness:

> And much as they say, "Well, oh, you're welcome to come with us," you always feel like the third person out. (June)

Perhaps the passive voice connotes their waiting to be invited, a pattern also prevalent among widows in Florida (van den Hoonaard 1994, 126-27). In that community, widows not only found that they had to wait to be invited to join couples in their frequent dinner excursions but they also had to follow "rules for survival" if they wanted to continue to be invited. These included going where the couple already decided to go rather than participating in the decision; paying for herself rather than letting the couple treat her to dinner; finding a "discreet" way of paying her bill rather than making it obvious that she was paying her own way; and putting on a good face rather than being "depressing" to be with. These "rules for survival" are indicative of the lower social status the women had as widows compared with the status they enjoyed as one half of a couple (Lopata 1975).[4]

Not everyone had this problem with all their friends. Nancy had close, long-time friends with whom she continued to feel comfortable:

> Now my friends from S.... it was just as natural for me to be with them to go somewhere to do something as it had been when we would all four of us go. But there are some people that make a real difference ... that hurts.

In addition to the feeling of discomfort, some women found that certain activities were no longer possible. For example, Doris, her husband and another couple had often played cribbage and other games that require a foursome together. Although the emotional ties between Doris and that couple remain strong, some of their leisure activities are no longer possible because they are now three rather than four.

All of the above aspects of the couples' world contributed to most women's feeling excluded from it:

> I know that there's always going to be parties ... that we used to go to that I'm not going to be included.... I tell you, it's a couples' world. (Eileen)

A widow is an extra woman and "nobody wants an extra woman around" (Judy). Even when the extra woman was included, she might be forgotten. Emily said that sometimes when she was out with couples, somebody would suddenly say, "Oh, Emily's here," as if she had been overlooked.

But widows are not always overlooked. The other side of that coin, noticed by many widows and found in almost all studies regarding widowhood, is the extra woman as a threat. Judy had thought that being older would have mitigated the fear that some women seem to have that widows are after their husbands, but she was mistaken. For some this added a contrived feeling to interaction as they had to be very careful in their actions lest they be misinterpreted.

Audrey was warned by an older woman to "be careful" because she had become a threat to couples. She calls it "part of this couple business." When Audrey's husband first died, many of her friends were very "huggy and affectionate," but she soon realized that women felt she was dangerous. This created a particularly difficult situation for Audrey because she had always enjoyed talking to men more than to women:

> I can be friends with a man quite easily, and so you miss that.

Audrey would have also liked to start a business, for which the most likely clients would have been single men. She decided against this because she felt that this would have been interpreted as her being in the market for a husband.

## Conclusion

The material in this chapter highlights the challenges widows have in try-ing to find comfortable and successful ways to maintain relationships with their friends. They recognize that the prerogatives of the emotional role of grief, which confers the right of being excused for "public displays of feelings that might otherwise be hidden" (Averill and Nunley 1988, 86), do not last very long. Accordingly, the women work very hard to keep up the appearance of not being too overwhelmed with grief in order to sat-isfy their friends, their husbands and themselves that they are succeeding in their adjustment to widowhood and that it will not make their friends uncomfortable to be with them.

Nonetheless, the lack of clear norms makes it difficult for women and their friends to negotiate the obligations involved in their relation-ships successfully. As well, the widows find that a single woman does not fit in socially either in private spheres like dinner parties or in public places like resort hotels and restaurants.

Being alone in a couples' world can be very uncomfortable. Learning to interact with men in new ways can seem insurmountable. The next chapter will look at how women approach this challenge and to what extent they master it.

## Notes

1 Note the change of term from "friend" to "acquaintance" that Emily makes in this quotation from her interview. As I discuss later in the chapter, this reinter-pretation of the nature of a relationship may be quite common among the mar-ried friends of widows.

2 See Hochschild (1973) for a discussion of the "sibling bond," based on reciprocity and similarity of situations, which developed among a group of widows living in a subsidized apartment building.

3 Laurel L. Smith (1991), in her qualitative study of older widows, also reports frequent use of the term couples' world, which she interprets as highlighting widows' feeling of being in a deviant state.

4 In fact, some of the widows I interviewed in Florida were quite judgmental about those who did not seem to understand their new status. For example, one woman was very resolute in her assessment of a new widow who was upset that her friends did not consult her about where to go out to dinner together. This widow insisted, "When you go with the widows, you make up your mind, but when you go with a couple, you're not going to tell them where to go. They're the ones that are doing you a favour and taking you. That's the way I feel, and maybe that's the reason I get along so nice with people" (van den Hoonaard 1994, 126).

# Chapter 5

# Relationships with Men

*A*s challenging as relationships with friends and adult children were for these women, those with men were even more complicated and ambiguous for these widows. As wives, they had known how to act with their husbands and with men who were either single or married. Once they found themselves single, they had to decide whether or not they were interested in getting married again. Even if they did not want to remarry, they had to figure out new ways to interact with men, both to avoid being misunderstood and because norms regarding relationships between unmarried men and women have changed in the twenty, thirty or fifty years since they had had to deal with them.

### Attitudes towards Remarriage

Most women did not want to get married again. In fact, out of twenty-three, fifteen stated categorically that they had no interest in remarriage. Four thought they might like to remarry, and four were not sure how they felt about the issue.[1]

Very few women had talked to their husbands about the possibility of remarriage. Of the few who did, only one man had told his wife that he preferred her not to marry again. The other women who had discussed the issue with their husbands had all got their "permission" to remarry.

---

Notes to chapter 5 are on p. 87.

Widows had several reasons for not wanting to get married again. Most common was the belief that they had already had the best possible husband and would find themselves constantly comparing a new husband with someone else:

> It would be completely unfair. I'd be comparing all the time. (Peg)

> Nobody could walk in his shoes. (Eileen)

Muriel went so far as to tell me that she would find herself looking for someone who was exactly like her husband:

> Very rarely you're going to meet the second one that's going to have ... the [same] mannerism and speech and things like that.

Marie, who had only been widowed a few months, told me that her husband was "the perfect man." In fact, she seemed to recognize that he had some faults—but for *her* he was the perfect man.

Peg felt that she would not only be comparing two men, but would also be comparing two times of life. Nothing could come close to her "young, romantic marriage." She could not visualize a new husband bringing her "flowers and things like that" the way her first husband had.

Although two women said that they would like to remarry because of having had a good experience the first time, it was more common for women to feel that it was too risky to imagine that they might have another experience that was as good:

> When you've had a wonderful marriage for forty-seven years, you would never risk it again. (Lynn)

Of the few women who stated that they would be interested in marrying again, Doris and Blanche felt that they had had such a good experience the first time that a second experience would also be good. Emily felt that marrying would provide companionship, and Audrey thought marrying again would help her deal with the loneliness she felt after a good marriage.

Second, some women either felt that they had already suffered enough with losing one or sometimes two husbands already, or they did not want to compromise their way of living again. Sylvia, for example, had already lost two husbands, both suddenly—one in an accident and the other from a massive heart attack. She simply felt that she could not take another loss on that scale. Others, for example Marilyn, had suffered through their husbands' long illness and felt that, although it might sound selfish, "I don't want to go through that again," and Edith felt that she'd "rather be alone than go through all that agony again."

Third, although all but one woman claimed to have had excellent marriages, a number recognized that they had compromised or scheduled their lives around their husbands in ways that they really did not care to repeat with someone whom they would not love as much. Peg has found that she wants her "space" (referring primarily to physical space). Sharon remarked:

> And I'm quite contented the way I am. I am my own boss here and [can] come and go [as I please].

Marion, who thought that she might remarry, was quite specific in stating that a prospective husband would both have to like music and to like the same kind of music she liked, for she had been unable to listen to *her* music around her husband because they had had different tastes—they had listened to the types of music he had preferred.

Marital roles have changed considerably in the last twenty years. These women had, for the most part, carried out the "traditional" female roles of taking primary responsibility for cooking and housecleaning. Lydia recognized that times have changed. She had "catered" to her husband—cooking his meals, cleaning the floor and the stove, having meals ready *when* he wanted them. She came to feel that men are more messy. She was not willing to repeat this pattern with someone new, even though she felt that the days when gender roles in marriage were more clearly delineated had been a time when people were happier together. Muriel went so far as to comment that men who wanted to get married were probably "looking for someone to look after them.... I sure wouldn't take on another!"

Fourth, some women continued to feel a deep attachment to their husbands. Cathy wondered how she could possibly consider remarriage when she was "still crying." This feeling of loyalty and connection to their husbands had an impact on various areas of life discussed elsewhere, for example, in decision-making. Lydia, Edith and Marie felt such a strong tie that they each commented that they were "still married." This, in fact, was the reason they gave me for not removing their wedding rings.

### The Symbolic Meaning of Wedding Rings

For many women, an important sign of loyalty and connection was their continuing to wear their wedding rings. Wedding rings reinforced a sense of connection to one's husband, symbolized one's refusal to consider remarriage and functioned as a protection against unwanted approaches by men who might think that one was *available*.

Widows' wedding rings often helped them to maintain their feeling of closeness with their husbands. They said they would "wear it forever"

(Judy) and would feel terrible if they ever had to take it off. For Sylvia and Judy the fact that their husbands had put their wedding ring on their finger reinforced this sense of connection.

Many widows interpret taking off one's wedding ring as an indication that she is willing to remarry.[2] In fact a number interpreted my question about their continuing to wear their wedding ring as a question about remarriage. For example, when I asked Lynn if she would keep her wedding ring on for the rest of her life, she told me:

> Oh, no, I won't touch them. I have no interest in ever getting married again.

Illness forced Emily to cut her wedding ring off, and she was concerned that an acquaintance might misinterpret her action both as disloyalty and, perhaps, an interest in another man:

> I had to go to a stranger. I couldn't go to anybody I knew.

Wedding rings also act as a defence against others either knowing that a woman is a widow or thinking that she is interested in a relationship:

> I don't think there'd be any use of letting people know I was available. (Frances)

> Well, suppose someone else comes along, if a man comes along and sees you have your wedding band, he's not going to approach you. (Eileen)

Marion, who had to take her wedding ring off because it no longer fit, wears other rings on her left hand as a protection against unwanted advances.

Only four women had taken their rings off voluntarily. Muriel had never worn hers when she was married. She and her husband had joked about others thinking she was "available." The others were not averse to remarriage.[3]

Although most women did not find the decision to keep their wedding ring on difficult, there also seems to be some ambiguity in the norms surrounding this issue. Thus, Doris was still wearing her ring, but asked me what I thought she should do. Some women reported that others had told them that they should remove their rings and that this had brought home to them the fact that they really were widows.[4]

Eleanor's experience with removing her wedding ring exemplifies the dilemma some women face. She indicated a willingness to remarry and was involved with a man. She initially took off her wedding ring when she and this man were going out for dinner with another couple: "I felt he would be embarrassed." She was not convinced that she had made the right decision in removing her wedding ring. Although she sometimes still wore the ring, she took it off whenever they were going to be in public together:

> I just felt ... as staid as he is and being the way he is, that he wouldn't be comfortable.

Eleanor's son noticed immediately that she had removed the ring. It was a problem for him, and Eleanor wrestled with her own reaction to her son's disapproval:

> And then I think, "Why do I have to make excuses to my children?"

She continued to leave the ring off because it made her friend more comfortable and because "it doesn't change how much I loved [my husband]."

Nonetheless, Eleanor asked me if I thought she had made the right decision, even though she recognized the risk that she was sending a message that she was available. In the end she concluded that

> And we can ... pick up the pieces and make a life, or we can wallow in it and be miserable and make everybody else miserable.

Even though she still wore her wedding ring, Mimi stated that she had not had a satisfying marriage. She was more than happy to be on her own and felt more free. For her the risk of becoming involved in another bad marriage was simply so great that she referred to it as "another bondage." Her wedding ring protected her from others thinking that she might be willing to enter into another marriage.

### Cautionary Tales about Second Marriages

Whether or not they wanted to remarry, these women did not believe in getting married "just for the sake of it" (Marion). Perhaps Frances's comment sums their attitude up best:

> Marry in haste, repent at leisure.

There were so many stories about unhappy second marriages that one might consider these "cautionary tales" (Hochschild 1989). Cautionary tales are stories told among a group in order to warn them against an activity that might be dangerous to them. Many fairy tales would qualify as cautionary tales—for example, *Hansel and Gretel*, which alerts children to the dangers of talking to and taking candy from strangers who might not be what they seem.

Sharon told a story that was typical of others. It has the requisite second marriage, the disastrous consequences and two unhappy families:

I guess I saw A's sister, she got married the second time, and it was devastating ... a lot of hardship because you have two families.... [Second marriages] are harder.

Frances was unable to recall a specific story, but remarked that "you hear of it, your friends talk about someone." The fear of again having to watch someone die showed up in some of these stories:

His wife died of cancer.... But he got married again, and his wife has got cancer. Just found out last week, his second wife has cancer. (Edith)

Eleanor told me of a man who "flew" into a second marriage and whose new wife suffers from manic depression. These tales are the stuff of nightmares. Regardless of whether they had a cautionary tale to relate, the sense that a second marriage might be risky was a general one.

### Negotiating Relationships with Men

Although they showed very little inclination to become romantically involved, these widows did communicate a desire for male company, whether simply for the companionship or for physical, albeit not intimate, contact.

Sylvia and June expressed a desire to have someone to go out with. June put it this way:

Just to go out for dinner ... and dancing for a few hours ... and then you just go home and you've had a lovely evening and look at my husband's picture up there on the wall and I think it's a nice night's adventure.

Women like Audrey missed the type of conversation they have with men. She commented that she actually preferred conversations with men to those with women. Audrey thought that, although she could easily be friends with a man, that it was likely he would misunderstand the intent. He might think:

You're looking for a husband, and that's not necessarily it—it's nice just to have a friend.

Both women and men often think that a cross-gender friendship implies romance, courtship and an intimate sexual relationship (Adams 1985).

Several women commented that they would like male companionship for the physical contact. Only a few brought up issues of sexual intimacy. For most, this simply referred to hugging.

Three women, all in their fifties, spoke specifically about missing sexual intimacy. Audrey said:

Even the sex thing, I mean, I found that hard, really lonely ... sexual desire ... and no way of fulfilling that.

June, whose husband had Alzheimer's disease, commented that she had been faithful to her husband, but that they had not had a sexual relationship for some time because of his illness. She said that she

> didn't miss that ... like some women might if their husband just died suddenly. Because I didn't have it for so long.

For the few who did comment on issues of intimacy, the changing mores regarding sex provided a challenge. Going out with a man for the first time could be "traumatizing." Marion and Audrey both remarked that they had felt like an adolescent again at the "first beginnings of some sort of physical relationship." When these women were growing up, intimate relationships were, for the most part, confined to marriage, and, although a couple were almost apologetic about their "outdated" moral standards, they were not about to "crawl into bed with somebody" (Emily) because "there has to be a relationship." As Eleanor commented:

> And I don't believe in jumping in bed with every man that comes along.

There was some recognition that men might not share this reluctance to engage in a sexual relationship on a casual basis. This was a cause for concern. Edith, for example, had gone out to dinner with someone thinking that they were going to "go out and just talk." The man she was with wanted her to

> go around with him, go away with him and all that—you wouldn't imagine that at our age, but he did.

She went on to state that men are different from women in this regard. Living together without marrying was also not a viable option for these widows.

A safer avenue for physical contact was hugging.[5] Martha and Sharon relied on specific men at their church for hugs. The safety of the Sunday service setting was underlined for both of them by the fact that these hugs took place in the presence of the men's wives and were so obviously harmless that nobody found them a threat:

> Like B. and I, we'd never think anything of it, we'd start hugging each other up [at church], but [his wife] is such a sweetheart. (Sharon)

June had found a safe environment in formal ballroom dancing. Studios provide a partner, and it is understood that "you don't date anybody or anything." Her dancing provided her a place where she could

> dance with someone and I think I'm dancing with my husband.

For this reason she only frequented the better studios and avoided public dances.

Conversely, some noted that they were careful to arrange their relationships in such a way as to avoid gossip. Peg has "very strict rules" about when male visitors leave her house at night because she lives in a small town where she feels others would notice and comment on late-night visitors. Sharon reported that a friend told her that she couldn't have ministers visit her alone because of the impression that would make. Her reaction was "garbage." A friend who was also a minister and she laughed about it when they were alone, but her friend had been serious. Audrey commented that Rivertown was small enough that if "you showed up at market on Saturday morning, it means you slept together Friday night."

Even though they went to great lengths to avoid misunderstandings, the women felt that many married women considered them a threat. This has been a constant finding in research on widowhood and is, therefore, not surprising. Some men, particularly single men, also assumed that widows were interested in them and reacted as if they were threatened. For example, Marion said that

> if you bake bread or give them something, they get ... all nervous. And I just think it's nice to do something nice for people.... I have to be very careful not to overwhelm them, I guess.

Some simply felt they have to disabuse men of the assumption that they were interested in more than conversation or companionship.

The motives of men were also problematic. Two contrasting stories highlight this difficulty. First, Audrey told me the story of a phone call she received from a man who had seen her at the cemetery when she was visiting her husband's grave. He had been visiting his wife's grave. This man was interested in getting together. Audrey's reaction was to avoid him:

> He's hurting and he's lonely ... but I'm not going to encourage anything here.

In this case, Audrey's guess about the man's motives were probably correct.

Marilyn, on the other hand, also received attention from a man who noticed her at the cemetery. When he approached her and started up a conversation, she made the same assumption Audrey had made, and her reaction was almost identical: "I felt sorry for him." It turned out that the man had seen some young men with beer bottles in the area the night before and was simply warning her to be careful:

> I immediately jumped to the conclusion he was going to come there and meet me the next night.... And I thought, "Isn't it a riot that you jump to these conclusions."

Both women felt vulnerable and uncertain because of the new basis on which they were meeting and interacting with men. They jumped to conclusions about the men's intentions, one seemingly inferring his intentions correctly, the other incorrectly.

### Significant Relationships

Although most widows did not want to remarry and few reported having a more-than-superficial relationship with any men, there were three women who did have a relationship that was important enough to them that it came up over and over again during our interview in response to varied questions.[6]

Audrey was at the point of having to make a decision about whether to move towards remarriage. The situation was difficult, both because her male friend has emotional "baggage that he has to get rid of" and because of others' reactions to the relationship. Her story did not resemble the story of a young woman's looking towards a first marriage with innocent excitement. Rather she was dealing with divorce and AIDS, as well as the cautionary tales she had heard about second marriages.

Eleanor, who also thought that she might someday remarry, was involved with a slightly younger man who had never been married. The relationship dominated her thoughts so that almost any question I might ask ended up with conversing about some aspect of their relationship. They were the victims of matchmakers:

> Our best friends think it would be wonderful if we could get together;

gossip:

> There's one lady who has decided to make it her business to see if she can get us anywheres together;

and her children's reactions to her seeing this man so steadily:

> [My son] is downright ignorant about it.... And it wouldn't have mattered if it had been Jesus, himself come back, [he] would not have liked him because nobody's ever going to take his father's place.

The inhibiting effect of adult children may be significant in women's ideas about remarriage. For instance, Wu (1995, 729) notes that the incidence of remarriage among widows with adult children is 93 percent lower than for women without children.

Nonetheless, it was gossip that was most disturbing to Eleanor. She was concerned enough about it to refrain from attending her friend's church because of the inferences others would make. She also declined membership on civic committees that might link the two of them together.

Sharon also had a male friend with whom she spent a great deal of time, but, unlike both Eleanor and Audrey, she had no intention of ever remarrying, and made that quite clear to me. [7] She was one of the few widows who had developed a more-than-superficial relationship with a man in a way that was comfortable to them both. She related that she had made it quite clear that she had no intention of remarrying or living together from the outset of their relationship. Indeed, she was the only one of these three who still wore a wedding ring.

Sharon's relationship allowed her and her friend to talk to each other about their late spouses.[8] They went for walks, out to supper and took short trips together. Sharon believed that they were meant for each other at this point in their lives to fulfil a need. In fact, she had asked her husband to "look after" her from the next world and thought that her male friend might be her husband's way of making sure that she was all right. Nonetheless, Sharon felt guilty after their first supper together.

The friendship was very important to both Sharon and her companion. She needed someone to talk to other than her family. He also needed someone who would be willing to listen to his talking about how much he missed his wife. In fact, Sharon read me a note from her friend in which he wrote that he did not know how he would have gotten by without her friendship and sympathetic ear.

Sharon's sons were very supportive of her relationship, "100 percent," while her friend's daughters were more cautious. Sharon thought that the difference was probably because daughters are more sensitive than sons. Others, who were not members of her family, also reacted to the liaison, not always positively. Some thought she was going out too soon, while others may have been jealous of the fact that she had a steady man to go out with regularly. Sharon concluded that they might eventually go their separate ways. They were the right people at the right time for each other, but marriage was not in their future.

## Concluding Thoughts

The material in this chapter once again demonstrates that widows have to reconstruct ways to interact with others, in this case with men. If the men are married, widows have to be careful not to give their wives (and sometimes the men themselves) the wrong impression. If the men are single, the widows again have to figure out ways to deal with them in ways that do not send a message they do not want to send—hence the significance of the wedding ring as a symbol of fidelity to their late husbands.

As well, they have to learn to interpret approaches from men. They tend to flee from advances because they do not always know how to construe them. Even if they are interested in remarriage, they are faced with changed sexual mores, suspicious children and men who think that everyone is after them.

After fifty, sixty or seventy years of acting in ways that felt natural, widows have to behave in ways that seem artificial. They have to anticipate others' new reactions to whatever they do. The rules have changed, and they don't know the new ones; these have to be learned, often by trial and error. Thus, they may find themselves out to dinner with someone who expects the evening to include intimate sexual contact when they envisioned only pleasant conversation.

There is no comfort level. This life is very different from the one they had left.

### Notes

1  In fact, widows over fifty-five are unlikely to remarry. DiGiulio (1989, 130) found that only 5 percent of widows over fifty-five remarry, although he also found that only 47 percent were unwilling to remarry.
2  I also found this in an earlier study of the experience of being widowed in a Florida retirement community (van den Hoonaard 1994).
3  In fact, two had remarried at the time of this writing.
4  See chapter 2 for a discussion of identifying moments.
5  A younger widow in her forties told me that she gets massages from male massage therapists in order to get the "male touch" in a safe way.
6  As Becker (1970) noted long ago, the evidential value of statements, which are volunteered rather than directed by a question from the researcher, is very strong. Two of these three women brought up issues about their relationships with men in response to a variety of questions, many seemingly not connected to these associations. It is clear that these were of great concern to them.
7  In fact, she was so categorical in her denial of romantic interest that my impression was that she had a difficult time convincing others of her intent.
8  Usually both women and men talk to women about their emotional suffering at this time.

# Part Three

## Discovering New Paths

# Chapter 6

## I Never Knew I Could ...

*B*ecause of the tremendous loss involved, one usually thinks of widowhood primarily or even solely in negative terms. How much less income does a widow have? To what extent is her health negatively affected? Does she lose all her friends? But growth is also an intrinsic part of widowhood for most women. The ability to cope and to learn to do new things comes as a surprise to many women. This chapter will focus on what women said about learning to do new things, living alone, driving and taking care of or buying a new car and the changes in self-concept that have accompanied these accomplishments.

### Learning to Do New Things

When I asked women if there was anything about the experience of being a widow that had surprised them, the most frequent answers revolved around emotional strength and the unexpected ability to learn how to do new things.[1] Sharon, for example, had expected to "go to pieces" if her husband died. She commented that she had done "real well." Others expressed this in stronger terms. Their husbands' deaths had really seemed like the end of their world. They had not been able to "envision going on alone" (Doris). Even surviving had been a surprise to Marion, and Sarah had expected to be a "basket case."

Notes to chapter 6 are on pp. 101-102.

Some found out that they enjoyed taking over some of the decision-making responsibilities. Marion found that her "personality came out more," while Blanche simply commented that she enjoyed "making the rules." Part of this was learning to be more assertive, to be able to say no.

Martha, for example, reported that a neighbour had wanted to buy a piece of property adjacent to her own. Because there had been trouble with this neighbour in the past, she told the man that she did not think this was a good idea. What surprised her was her own assertiveness:

I thought I was a baby [but] I wasn't afraid to give my opinion.

She felt that, in the past, she would have gone along with her neighbour and later regretted it.

The ability to do new things also came as a surprise to many women. Several had lists of things they had not been able to do in the past. For example, Muriel had learned to drive, learned to work her VCR, built a stone wall, painted a fence and planted a garden. Some of these tasks were not momentous, but they represented victories that contributed to feelings of competence and confidence. The way Muriel told the story of learning to use her VCR underlined the extent of the achievement:

The electricity had gone out and the clock was "blinking, 12:00, 12:00.... I never adjusted that thing, and I didn't even know how to open the little box there." Because she was intimidated, she let the light blink on and off for a week. Then, "I put a book up so I wouldn't see it ... and said I don't know how to do it." Finally, Muriel decided, "I'm going to fix this thing or it's going to be unplugged." She got the instructions out and went step by step until it was done. For many people this may seem like a minor accomplishment, but for Muriel it was "a big achievement."

The challenge of learning to program and work with a VCR symbolizes the obstacles that their houses present to many widows. It is an everyday appliance, which has become a threatening stranger—one that may constantly reinforce in their minds the effort it now takes simply to live in their houses. As the light blinks on and off, it heckles them with the constant reminder that here is something they cannot handle. When they finally face this enemy, widows discover they can overcome a barrier that had previously seemed insurmountable.[2]

In addition, the women learned that they were capable of doing some household jobs they would previously have left to their husbands. Peg was surprised at how good she was with a hammer and nails, while Audrey discovered that she could do simple repairs. Even those who still needed to hire people to take over some of their husbands' chores found they could do a few unexpected tasks. For example, Lydia was the proud owner of a black-and-blue thumb she received as a product of her first attempt at hammering. She bruised her thumb, but she got the job done: "It's the first thing, but it's surprising."[3]

### Living Alone

Although it is most often the choice of women to live alone after the loss of their husbands (Doyle et al. 1994), some women found that their ability to do this was the biggest surprise. Doris, for example, remarked that although she did not like living alone, the fact of being able to stay alone came as a pleasant surprise. Martha noted that she really had not known if she would be able to live alone. She had been afraid she might have had to

> give it up and go into an apartment or something.

Sharon's "biggest fear" had been coming to the house when it was empty. When she arrived home, she found herself wondering "who's in the house." She recounted her experience of a feeling that her husband said to her as she unlocked the door one day:

> "Mom, you're gonna be all right."

This led to her overcoming her fears, and she reported that she was no longer afraid to enter her own house. Coming home to an empty house is difficult for many women. M. T. Dohaney (1989), in her autobiographical account of her first year of widowhood, wrote that it took her six months to realize that if she turned on the lights before leaving, she would not have to come home to a dark house later.

Living alone was a new experience for most widows. Of twenty-eight, only seven had lived alone before: three because they had married late, one as a widow, one when she was divorced and two who commented that it had been for a short time. Five, who had never lived alone, had spent time alone with their children because their husbands travelled as part of their work. Seven women noted that they had moved from their parents' homes to live with their husbands when they married.

June, whose husband had had Alzheimer's disease, said that she had "lived pretty well alone.... I was married, yet I wasn't married" even before her husband died. She had lived in a state of "quasi-widowhood" (Rosenthal and Dawson 1991, 317). In this situation:

> women find themselves still married yet living alone and in many respects without the mate they once had.

Many responsibilities had fallen on her shoulders gradually as her husband's condition deteriorated, with his finally entering a nursing home.[4]

Living alone presented particular challenges. First was simply the fear of being in the house alone. Eileen commented that she heard "more noises and more ... wood cracking or the windows or whatever." Both Marilyn and Audrey thought that my question of living alone was really about being afraid. Marilyn had married when she was forty-six and had, therefore, lived alone for a number of years prior to her marriage. When I commented on this, she replied:

> Yeah, like I have never been afraid to stay alone, and I admit I have no patience with those who are.... If I'm nervous, it's nervous of something real. But I don't think about people breaking in.[5]

Audrey responded to my question of whether or not she had lived alone before this way:

> I'm not afraid to be alone. I feel very comfortable out here [in a suburban subdivision]. I've got wonderful neighbours here.... I mean I think I'm safer and less at risk of my house being broke into and everything out here than I am in town.

Lydia was not afraid to live alone, but she did take precautions:

> As long as things are secure and I've got blocks of wood in the doors and things, it doesn't bother me.

She also had a boarder and a dog, both of whom have increased her a sense of security.

Many had anticipated that living alone would be one of the most important challenges they would face. They felt that if they gave in to the temptation to stay with others, or have others stay with them while their husbands were ill or just after they died, they might never get the courage to attempt staying alone in their houses. Martha had allowed her daughters to spend the first four nights with her after her husband died, but when the four nights were up and they wanted her to stay with one of them, she said:

> "No, I have to stay here, I've got to face it. If I'm going to live in my own home, I've got to face up to it.... I will stay here." So I did from then on.[6]

Sarah had begun to prepare herself while her husband was in the hospital. Her children had wanted to stay with her, but

> I wouldn't let them; I was preparing myself.

Doris forced herself not to stay with friends "in town" because

> I'm not old enough to have someone stay with me forever, and I'm not old enough to go somewhere else for the rest of my life, so I have to stay here. So I did, but it was not easy

These women insisted on staying alone because they were afraid that if they did not bite the bullet, they might put it off forever. Eleanor had a cautionary tale to share:

Because a couple my age live up in the house ... and her father died, and every night her mother goes to her house, and now she's too old; she stays there all the time. But at that time, every morning at twenty to eight, she went down the road with her Save-Easy bag, with her nightgown in it. And I said, "I will not be coming home with my bag with my nightgown in it every morning. I've got to do this; I've got to learn to deal with it. I've got to learn to be alone."

And she did.

It is interesting to note that several of the women felt that, had they died first, their husbands would not have been able to cope without them. As much as they missed their husbands, they did not feel they would have been able to cook or clean properly for themselves. This is reinforced by the reactions of widowers I interviewed in a Florida retirement community. Several men said that they "could not live alone" (van den Hoonaard 1992). Although women may not like living alone, it is rare to hear one say that she *cannot* live alone.

The issue of whether widowhood is more difficult for men or women is still being debated. Berardo (1970), for example, has argued that widowhood is harder for men because not only do they not know how to do household chores, but he also felt that they would not get the same feeling of esteem by mastering "women's work" as women get from mastering chores that they had left to their husbands. Kate Davidson (1995), in a study comparing the experience of widows and widowers, found that both men and women cite missing their spouse as their biggest problem, but feel that the biggest problems for the opposite sex would be practical ones.

### Driving

Another area of life that presented difficulty for some widows concerned driving and taking care of their car. Fewer than half of the widows who participated in the study were completely comfortable with driving; they talked about "jumping" in the car when they were lonely, and seemed to simply take driving for granted. A number did remark, however, that they thought they were lucky that they knew how to drive and that others, who do not know, should learn how to drive.

Several women drove, but talked about it in a way that suggested that driving was not a natural or easy thing for them. Marion had had her license all along, but had "hated driving." She began driving regularly when her husband died and stated that

I don't drive any distance.... I get around town; I do the things that I need to do.

Her high-performance car needed to be "run hard once a month or so." She, therefore, regularly lent it to friends who took it out on the highway for her.

Eileen also reported that she only drove locally. She had difficulty with her sight and had begun to drive at night, which she had not done before. Her daughters were so worried about her driving alone that they wanted her to have a phone in the car. Her reaction was that it was too expensive and that she did not go very far with the car in any case.

Both Muriel and Edith had learned to drive recently, and for both it was an important accomplishment. Muriel had not previously driven at all, but she had felt that she had to learn to drive:

> I didn't drive at all, so I went out ... to Young Drivers with all these teenagers.... I learned how to drive the car.... It feels good, too, you know, nothing really spectacular.

Edith had known how to drive, but had never driven very much until her husband became ill and she had to drive him ninety minutes each way to have medical tests every week. Each step was a major accomplishment:

> So one day I said to [my son], "I drove over the bridge today." So he said, "So?" "Well to me that's something."

Several women had previously known how to drive, but no longer drove. Betty had driven when she and her husband lived in a small town, but had stopped when they moved to the city:

> I'm scared of this crazy town.

Her husband had done all the driving once they moved and had encouraged her to try:

> "Betty, you should try to drive up here, 'cause I'm not going to be able to much longer." And I'd say, "Yes, you're right.... I gotta learn in traffic." I never did, and then he was gone.

Sylvia had learned to drive when she was a young woman, but soon after that her husband had made a remark about her not scratching a new car they had bought and she "threw the keys [at her husband]" and never drove again. This has made her life especially difficult because she lives in a very small town and has become dependent on neighbours, who are not always available or willing to provide transportation.

Peg, who had stopped driving when her eyesight deteriorated, also lived in a small town and paid people who gave her drives. She had sold her car so that she would not be tempted to drive even though she could not see well enough. She felt that she would soon have to make a decision about where to live because, since small towns do not have public transportation, she could not remain there indefinitely.

Sarah had also known how to drive before she got married. She had made a conscious decision not to drive because she did not want to go places alone:

> I saw so many people going alone, their husbands would stay home and watch T.V. And if I wanted to go any place ... he would automatically take me.... And so I got used to him going with me that I thought, "I don't want him to throw the keys at me and say, 'Here, you go.' "[7]

Friends had encouraged Sarah to drive when her husband died, but her daughter told her that she would be too worried:

> "Mom, we've go enough worries with you living alone."

Sarah got rides from her daughter, her daughter's friends and lived right near a bus stop. She had no intention of ever driving again.

### Taking Care of the Car

Whether they were comfortable driving or not, those women who did drive soon discovered that they had to learn how to maintain their car. Repairs had routinely been taken care of by their husbands, and nobody claimed to have any mechanical knowledge regarding her car. Emily commented that she still didn't know anything about car maintenance. Lydia and Marion had both solved this problem by finding a good mechanic.

For Eleanor, remembering to do things like changing the oil in the car was a new responsibility that made her feel she had become a "stronger person." For Blanche taking care of the car became a burden:

> Drat, the car needs this or that, something's gone wrong.... You know, for fifty years, I've been able to say, "There's something that's not working right," and it gets done. And all of a sudden I've got to find the person who'll do it.

Edith, on the other hand, found that doing small things she had "dreaded," like taking her car to a car wash, gave her a feeling of increased confidence.

### Buying a Car

Clearly, cars represent an area that is foreign to most women. When they begin to master the tasks associated with owning and driving a car, they are moving into a realm that we still think of as belonging primarily to men. This becomes even more obvious when we look at what the four women who had recently bought a car had to say about that experience.

Judy had bought her new car while her husband was still living; therefore, he had gone along with her. She reported that the salespeople had walked right up to her husband and had ignored her, assuming that he, as the man, was the real buyer of the car. Finally, her husband had told the salesman:

"You better not come near me ... she's going to be angry.... I'm not buying the car; she is." But they go right to the men.

Emily had a similar experience, except that she went to buy her car alone. She felt that it was being an "ignorant woman" rather than specifically a widow that put her at a disadvantage when she went to buy a car. At first, "a lot of them wouldn't even talk to me" simply because she was a woman "and didn't know anything." Emily felt particularly vulnerable because she was trading in a Cadillac and had already had "a lot of challenges ... putting batteries in that didn't need to be in and doing all those things." Although she claimed that she still did not know anything about cars, Emily did manage to get a figure on a trade-in and did "learn quite a bit really." Nonetheless, Emily is not alone in feeling that people react to any woman by assuming that she is ignorant, particularly about cars, and that sales people and mechanics can, therefore, "lead [them] down a lane."

Eileen bought a new car to please her daughters, who had felt that they would worry about her if she were driving the older car even though, according to Eileen:

The car [was] working fine [although] it was six years old and they thought maybe it would break down.

When Eileen first went to buy her car, the salesman told her that he had nothing to sell her within her price range. She thought, "This bugger thinks this widow's not gonna...." She knew the owner of the dealership and called him to report her experience. She said that the salesman had since been laid off because of his brushing off women customers. Eileen also found the car she wanted, eventually, and drove a "hard bargain" on the price and inclusion of extras, i.e., a tape deck, in the previously agreed-upon price. She felt that one reason she was able to get what she wanted was because the dealer was surprised that a woman would bargain as she had done.

Unlike the others who bought a new car after their husbands died, Polly bought a used car. Her story represents the dependence some women have either on the honesty of dealers or on their family members to protect them from being "taken in" by unscrupulous dealers.

Polly bought a car she liked a lot and that was at the limit of the amount of money she had to spend on a car. She had picked out the car, and her son had gone with her to lay out the terms of what she wanted and to bargain with the dealer to lower the price. Polly would have paid the asking price because "I thought it was fair," but depended on her son to make sure the conditions were all right.

Soon after she bought the car, a panel light came on labelled, "check gauges." She took it back to the dealer who simply offered to take the car back if she didn't want it. But she was in a bind because, "Geez, you know, I really want this car; I really like this car." Her son trivialized the problem, remarking,

> "Why are you worrying about that light? I can't imagine why you would let a little thing like that bother you."

Polly's feeling was that a light comes on when something is wrong, but both the dealer and her son continued to downplay the problem while the dealer suggested it would cost her up to $2,000 to fix the light. When I interviewed Polly, she was still driving the car with the "check gauges light" sometimes coming on and sometimes not. It bothered her that something might actually be wrong, other than the loose wire that might be causing the light to come on, but the dealer told her:

> "Look, I'm not convinced that that's doing anything other than telling you to check your gauges" ... and I'm not prepared to pay twelve or fifteen hundred dollars for the repair of something that isn't broken.

All in all, just about all the women who participated in this study indicated that they had learned to do things they had not known they were able to do. Their sense of competence has grown, and, for some, has resulted in a change of their self-concept.

### Changes in Self-Concept

I asked each woman how she had changed since her husband had died, because in reading published autobiographical accounts of women's experiences of widowhood, I noticed that the authors had almost universally felt that they had changed to the extent of calling themselves "new women" (van den Hoonaard 1997).[8] The widows interviewed were more limited in their assessment of personal changes, perhaps because of their more advanced age. In fact, it seemed that several of the women interpreted "change" at their age as inevitably negative. For example, Eileen responded by saying:

> Not really, in the sense of change, no ... I'm not bitter.

Lydia's comments reflected the fact that she thought I was asking if she had changed in a negative fashion as well:

No, I don't think so. I've always tried to look on the bright side of life.... I still like to let my hair down ... no, I don't think I've changed.

Three women (Nancy, June and Florence) felt that they had not changed at all.

However, the women who did feel that they had changed since the death of their husbands focused more on interpersonal relations rather then on the chores they had mastered. The most common new trait that these women mentioned was an increased sense of empathy and compassion.

For Emily this meant being more sympathetic and understanding "for people that are alone." Her experience with losing her husband had made her realize that she had, like others, given unwanted advice to widows in the past. She learned that one cannot understand others' experiences until "you walked in their shoes." Sharon commented that she was able to "look back and see some of the stupid things I've said to people when somebody died." Now she felt she had "more to offer them," and Lynn said it made her "more aware of other people."

Judy remarked that her loss had made her "more caring with a deeper feeling for people that have lost their husbands." Although Doris did not feel that there were "actual changes," she did say that she had become "certainly more understanding of other people."

Other positive changes involved greater feelings of confidence and having become more outgoing. This was particularly evident for Eleanor, whose husband had been an amputee. Part of her approach to her marriage had been wanting "everybody to see how capable he was and what a strong person he was." Consequently, she had been "content to walk in his shadow." Because this was no longer necessary, she had become "more outgoing" as well as more confident "because of having to take on all of the responsibilities, like getting the oil changed in the car."

Blanche identified making decisions and following through on them as contributing to her feeling that she had become a stronger person. In addition, she said that she had learned to say no and "become a tougher character." Muriel and Marilyn also noticed that they had become more outspoken and assertive.

For Martha, becoming stronger had also meant increasing her religious faith. As she took on more that her husband had previously done, she had "relied on the Lord," overcome her fear and "grown much stronger being on my own."

Several women primarily identified negative changes. Three simply commented that they had aged or become older, while Betty noted that all she was doing was "worry, worry, worry" about money all the time. Only

Edith said that she had become bitter, although Marion found that she was disappointed in people.

Lynn, Sarah and Audrey mentioned that they found that they were doing more things for themselves. For example:

> I am spending more time for myself ... indulging myself. And if I want to go for a walk at a certain time, I don't have to answer to anyone, not that I had to answer to anyone, but you know, when you live with someone.... But maybe that comes with the territory, I don't know. Feeling guilty about it is something else, though. (Lynn)

This ambivalence about enjoying more personal freedom was a common theme in these women's experiences. Previously the rhythm of their lives had, to a large extent, conformed to their husbands' preferences. Now they only had to please themselves. Several commented that they had not felt constrained, but, nonetheless, they did notice this new freedom.[9]

## Concluding Thoughts

This chapter has looked at the breadth and number of new things that many widows have to accomplish as they learn to go on with their lives after their husbands' deaths. As their relationships need to find a new basis for continuing, so do women have to learn new ways to pick up the tasks that had previously been done by their husbands. Their mastery of these chores may lead to an enhanced level of confidence in themselves and the discovery of their capacity to be assertive and to make important decisions. One major area confronting widows, which I have not touched on in this chapter, is finance. The next chapter will look at the challenges women face with regard to reduced income levels as well as learning how to handle and make decisions about money.

### Notes

1 It is notable that most women interpreted this question in terms of positive surprises. It seems that they, too, did not expect anything positive to come out of their experience.

2 I have told the "VCR story" to many groups of women. A murmur of understanding always accompanies the recitation. In addition, in a focus group study on another topic, a related finding was that many households contained one "VCR expert." This is not usually the oldest woman in the house. Rather it is often her husband or one of her children if he or she still lives at home.

3 It should not be forgotten, however, that some of these efforts are by-products of reduced incomes rather than a real desire to master new skills.

4 June was the only woman whose husband had ended his life in a nursing home. A sample of women who had had this experience would probably present a different picture from the one painted by those whose husbands had spent their last days at home.

5 She is one of many women who have dogs and depend on them to communicate if something is wrong.

6 This is not a minor achievement. During the meeting of a support group for widows that I attended, the big news of the day was that one of the women had spent the previous night alone in her house. Her sister had been staying with her every night since her husband's death—six months earlier!

7 Sarah is one of two women who had consciously chosen not to learn a skill. The other is Marilyn, who specifically did not learn how to use the VCR and other appliances because she felt that, if she had, her husband would have stopped taking care of them and left that work to her.

8 Examples of these accounts are *Widow* by Lynn Caine (1974) and *When Things Get Back to Normal*, by M. T. Dohaney (1989).

9 I should note, however, that Polly felt quite uncomfortable even using the term freedom. After she had listed a number of ways in which she no longer had to conform to her husband's inclinations, I asked if there were other ways in which she felt more free. She backed up immediately: "I don't see it as freedom. I don't feel that I was oppressed before."

# Chapter 7

# And Speaking of Money

$T$his chapter will address financial issues faced by older women when they enter widowhood. It will first look at the change in their financial status, i.e., what they say happens to their income. It will then examine what women say about their knowledge of money and how they handle finances and make decisions about money. Finally, it will look at how attitudes towards money affect relationships with family and friends.

Research consistently shows that women's financial situations deteriorate when their husbands die and that unattached older women are among the poorest in Canada. Poverty rates among men and women 65 or over have dropped from 34 percent in 1980 to 19 percent in 1992. However, the rate for unattached women 65 or older was 45 percent in 1992 compared to 29 percent for unattached men of the same age. (National Council on Welfare 1994, 10, 16)[1]

The women who participated in this study were not representative of these figures. Although I did not directly ask them their income, most said that financially they were all right, and it was clear from their residences that most were comfortable. Nonetheless, one woman lived in sufficiently reduced circumstances that her rural home seemed to be deteriorating before my eyes, and a few lived frugally and may have been at or near the poverty level.

Whether poor or not, twenty of the widows reported that their income had been reduced by their husbands' deaths. Of the other seven,

---

Notes to chapter 7 are on pp. 115-16.

none of whom talked about the change in income, six seemed to have more than adequate financial resources and one seemed comfortable.

Simply noting reduced income does not really reflect how little or much income these women actually have. This is complicated by the sense of privacy we have about money in Canada. The only woman who gave me actual figures when I asked her how she is "doing financially" was also the only Native woman I interviewed. Her interview is notable for the frankness of her responses on many subjects. She is also one of the poorest women I spoke with.[2]

Ascertaining "objective" financial status is also difficult because, for the most part, the women I interviewed made a point of telling me that they were "making do" with the amount of money they now have. Sarah's comment is typical of those who seemed to be living quite frugally:

> There's a lot less money coming in, I can tell you that, that's a little hard, you have to, to learn to um ... watch what you're spending. But then you don't spend quite as much. (Sarah)

In fact, only two women appeared to have financial problems that they had difficulty handling.

Nonetheless, increased expenses often accompany the lower incomes. Many women now need to hire people to do some of the jobs their husbands used to do around the house:

> Everything that broke down, he would fix it. Now I have to send out for a plumber—thirty dollars an hour.... I'm no good at fixing things. (Edith)

> [My husband] was able to do everything and fix everything.... I have air conditioning, for example, ... having the air conditioners put in, you pay for somebody to put them in, you pay for somebody to take them out, and have the lawn mowed and snowblowing. And actually, my expenses have almost doubled. (Marilyn)

Marilyn also points out that her rent has gone up as well as power rates and other necessary expenses while her income was cut in half.

For most, "getting by" or "making do" characterizes the way they interpret their current financial situation. Eight women explicitly told me that they are getting by or making do because they are "on a strict budget" (Lydia), because they "don't care about monetary things" (Edith) or because they have successfully curtailed their activities. Edith may not care about monetary things, but she still reports having to give up some hobbies:

> [My sons tell me], "Oh, you should get painting again" ... but all these hobbies ... they're all expensive. And that's one thing I've found. Everything is

taken away from you when you become a widow.... When [my husband died] his pension from work—I didn't get it.

Others have given up or are no longer able to afford: concert tickets (Edith), holding office in a masonic organization (Lydia), house repairs (Martha) and sending Christmas cards (Florence). In addition, Martha reports that she now buys Christmas presents gradually throughout the year, and Florence sometimes buys her clothes and clothes for her mother-in-law, who is institutionalized, at yard sales. This generation of women, many of whom grew up during the Depression, "accepts hardship and suffering as an inevitable fact of life" (Cohen 1984, 131). It is, therefore, likely that they minimize the economizing they have had to do since their husbands died.

Sylvia stands out as the one woman who is not "getting by" and who blames herself for not being able to manage her money properly:

> I'm not the most, I was going to say I'm not frivolous or a spendthrift or anything, but I find it hard to juggle, you know, and make do. I go overboard more than I should and not being stupid, you know, I, I just buy too much food and I forget I'm alone.

Sylvia was not the only person who thought insurmountable money problems were related to a widow's inability to handle money rather than to the fact that she might simply just not have enough. Several women made remarks about women who overspend. For example:

> I find a lot of people, some of the widows that I know, they're not like real close friends, that they never looked after the money, and they just spent, spent, spent and they didn't have anything left.... They didn't have any sense of spending. (Sarah)

> But um ... I notice that there's a lot goes to bingo and they can't, you know, they're broke from one cheque to the next and so on and so forth. (Frances)

The sense that often women do not handle their income responsibly is consistent with assumptions that many women know very little about money and finance when they are married.

Previous research has found that women do not discuss their financial status with their husbands when they are dying (see, for example, Morgan 1986). This is another way in which my sample seems to diverge from the norm. Of twenty-four widows who gave the information, thirteen claimed that they had had the major responsibility for managing money in their marriage, seven said their husbands had taken most of the responsibility, three reported that they and their husbands had done it together and one woman stated that she and her husband handled their finances separately. These women still had the idea that many of their fellow widows did not know about money:

> Like I have friends who have no idea what their husbands earn, what they're, you know, what they owe, what they don't owe, and I think it's wrong. (Eileen)

> And I used to say over and over again ... "I don't know what happens to, you know, women whose husbands died and they've never made out a bank deposit or they don't know what on earth's going on." (Marilyn)

This ignorance is symbolized by the inability to write a cheque:[3]

> But I know there are some women who can't even write a cheque.... There were some women down at that grieving session at the hospital, you know. They couldn't write a cheque, carry money and things like that.... Some of them were really lost because they didn't know how to do anything. (Edith)

> I know my mother-in-law, she didn't even know how to write a cheque.... She never even had a cheque. He just gave her cash and she went and got groceries and that was it. (June)

> I feel so sorry for these people, they get left, and they don't know how to write a cheque. They don't know how to do their banking. They don't know how to pay their phone bill. (Eleanor)

> Like I have a friend whose husband died suddenly, she'd never written a cheque in her life. She had, didn't have a clue ... and it was dreadful for her. She had no idea how much money there was available, where it was and this on top of having all the emotional things to deal with is really, is really too much. (Marion)

Marion's comments are very telling because she is one of two women who took over the finances in their marriage after their husbands had been seriously ill and they had been terrified because they did not know anything about their financial situation. In fact, when I asked my respondents what advice they would give to people who are not widows, one of the most common answers was that wives should know how to deal with money and what their own situation is.

Although many of the women I interviewed said that they were familiar with finances or had actually been responsible for money matters, it is clear that issues surrounding money are not uncomplicated. Almost no research has been done that examines how money is allocated within families (Eichler 1988).[4] One study does note an important distinction between *managing* money and *controlling* money within a marriage (Edwards 1981). This study found that women often manage or share the management of money with their husbands, but husbands usually control or share the control with their wives. My respondents only spoke of *managing* the money in their marriage. I do not know which, if any, of the women who managed the money in their families also *controlled* it.

### Dealing with Money and Finance

Five subjects came up that are indicative of the challenges these women face when they deal with money and finance. They are: (1) the initial red tape involved with informing the government and others of their husbands' deaths; (2) the realization that they are now responsible for making decisions about money and for taking care of financial matters themselves; (3) their fears related to whether they will be able to handle the money and if there will be enough of it; (4) the reliance on financial advisors, whether family members or professionals; and (5) the impact of distrust and jealousy surrounding how well off they are in their relationships with friends and family, as well as the increased vulnerability they experience because they fear someone might take advantage of them because they are women.

When a spouse dies, there are many agencies, for example, Canada Pension, that the widow has to inform of his death. This must be done almost immediately and at a time when many women report feeling numb and bewildered.[5] Some funeral homes give out folders that have all the necessary forms in them as a service to the survivor, but many of the women I interviewed have no memory of ever seeing this package even though their husbands' funerals were handled by homes that do provide this service.

Often the bereaved spouse counts on a son, a brother or a daughter to "hold her hand" as she completes the many required forms. It is not uncommon for women to feel overwhelmed both by the amount of paperwork that needs to be done and by the inevitable red tape with which they have to deal:

> and then there are so many things that have to be done immediately after a person dies—so many things. Many of which are frustrating because you're dealing with the government. And um ... the experiences with the federal and the provincial governments were just absolutely exasperating. (Marilyn)[6]

> Right after, one of the hard things that you do have to do when you lose a spouse is you have to go around and do all this business right on top of the fact that you're really not with it. But my daughter came with me. (Peg)

> Right, exactly, and it's, and there's so many things you have to do when your husband dies, you can't, I couldn't believe it. But I was very fortu-

nate, and I had a brother that just kind of took over for me. And afterwards, you know, I thought, "Gee," quite a while afterward I thought, "Gee, I didn't do all those things, he went and did those." Like you have to let Canada Pension, and the Old Age Pensions and you had to make out, I didn't even know I had to make out an estate tax and he told me, he said, "You, you know, you have to do this, don't worry I'll look after it." (Judy)

There's an awful lot of stuff, business to look after when a man, when anyone dies today. 'Cause there was um ... there was the Old Age Pension, there was his Veteran's, there was a um ... Railroad, his, all his pensions were and um ... his Railroad pension was dropped immediately. (Florence)

When I asked Blanche whether she had vivid memories from the early days after her husband's death, she replied:

I think mainly being flooded with paper, things that have got to be decided, things that have to be signed, things that you've got to go down to the office and arrange about seemingly forever, um ... bills pouring in and you don't know where the money is, and ... trying to settle, get it all straight. Mostly those sorts of things.

It is dreadful, it really is absolutely dreadful. Especially the first month when they, they keep messing you about with these things. He died just before Christmas, well all this sort of had to be done somehow between Christmas and New Year because nothing was coming in. Half of the offices were closed, and people were away, and there wasn't anybody to certify whatever you said and you know, you've got to have somebody else and you've got to do this and you've got to do that, but, "Oops! we can't because it's New Year." (Blanche)[7]

As two of the women pointed out to me, the bureaucratic necessities are a nightmare for more than one reason. It is necessary for the widow to carry copies of her husband's death certificate with her so that she can produce it wherever she goes. This is emotionally draining:

There were letters to be written and you had, I don't know how many, you had to have, I don't know how many copies of his ... death, I said I carried, when they die, you carry that around in your purse for a month or more ... because everywhere you go they have to see it.

That is hard because you're carrying that thing in your purse all the time ... because if you go to the bank, if you go to um ... look after anything at all in the line of business you have to have that to show.... It just seems as though you're constantly showing somebody that he, that that person has died. (Florence)[8]

Once these women completed the bureaucratic necessities, the realization began to set in that they are now responsible for themselves financially. This is, of course, most striking if a woman did not participate in money management at all:

> It's my responsibility to look after myself now. I never had any responsibility of money. My husband always looked after that if I wanted something.... I'm the one that has to look after me now, and I've realized that since he's been gone. (Lydia)

Eleanor and her husband had shared management responsibility, but now she realized that "this is *all* your responsibility," while Sarah felt this most sharply when she was in a restaurant and realized that her husband was not there to pay for her meal:

> Because on Sundays, we always went out to a restaurant.... I realized I've got to pay for myself.... That was the hardest ... the first thing that happened. I thought, "Oh, I have to pay for this." ... You get used to it after a while.

For some, this new individual responsibility is accompanied by fear, whether it is because the previously joint responsibilities are now solely theirs, because their husbands had made the decisions about investments or simply because they are afraid they will run out of money. Doris commented:

> We would discuss something we were going to do and decide what's the best move.... But now I think it through a dozen times and say ... which is right and which is wrong.... I'm thinking different things with the house, about insurance.... It's so much more difficult in that respect.

Investments are particularly threatening because if you make the wrong decision, you can lose a great deal. Betty's husband had made some poor decisions about investments, and her memory of that coloured her ideas about investments. She remarked:

> I'm scared to death of stocks. [My husband] had stocks one time and nearly lost it.

Judy's fears were based on well-publicized stock scandals, and she was afraid to get caught in one:

> But it's scary ... look what happened to the Confederation Life people.... That amount of money would be difficult for me if I lost it.... I'd have to go into a senior citizen's place, I suppose.

Both Judy and Marie simply worried whether or not there would be enough money. Judy's fears were provoked by the large number of financial outlays that she needed to make right after her husband's death. It gave her the feeling that "everything was just going." Marie fretted about whether she would have enough money to get through the first year. She finds herself being very careful with every penny she spends.

In the past, credit card companies simply cancelled joint credit cards and often refused credit to a new widow who, in their eyes, had no credit history.[9] Although this practice has been moderated to some extent, credit card companies still complicate women's lives when their husbands die. Polly told me of going shopping and suddenly discovering that her credit cards had been cancelled when they were not accepted at the cash register. A collection agent called her and demanded that she pay off the $900 owing on one of the cards immediately. She told him that she did not have that much money but that she would continue to pay off the card gradually as she always had done. He wanted to know if her children could give her the money. Then, when she said that she was a widow, the agent offered to have the credit card company erase the debt that she had been willing to pay off gradually.

This story is in contrast to Mimi's experience. She cancelled all the credit cards but one when her husband died. The one she kept had a large balance of which she had been unaware. She now is stuck paying off this balance gradually. Although one cannot generalize from two stories, I cannot help but wonder if the difference in the credit card companies' responses to a similar situation is the fact that Mimi is Native.

There were two experiences that were quite different. Both were the result of professionals helping the women with the paperwork that had to be done. The first was reported by Muriel, who happens to be the widow of a retired member of the RCMP. When I asked her how she had known what paperwork needed to be done, she replied:

> All the correspondence came to me from the RCMP in Ottawa, so I would give it to [my husband's financial advisor] and he filled out all the papers and everything ... insurances and anything pertaining to the provincial government.... He looked after everything. And he would come and look for ... I would just stick everything in a drawer.... There was only one place I did go was Canada Pension.... And that was the only thing that I could safely say that I did on my own.

Muriel went on to point out that the RCMP just automatically phoned and sent someone over, paid for her husband's funeral and automatically gave her whatever she was entitled to:

> There's certain people that um ... that's all they do, that's their job, sit behind a desk and coordinate these things.[10]

Blanche reported that her husband's financial advisor took care of everything that needed to be done. She is certain she would not have been able to accomplish all the bureaucratic requirements without him:

> And I had no idea what I was supposed to do, and I knew that [the financial advisor] knew about a lot of these things, and I phoned him and he came to

the house. He helped. Without him, I don't know what I would have done.... You don't know what to do. You simply don't know what to do, and you need someone to help you.... It's difficult because you don't get any pension, you know, you don't get this, you can't do that, you can't do anything unless you, you get these papers signed off.

Blanche continues to use a financial advisor because of her sentiment that the money is not really hers:

I still feel it's his money, and I've got to spend it sensibly and wisely and look after it.... I don't entirely feel it's mine yet.... I'm only allowed to use it, but it isn't mine. It's hard to explain.

Other women continue to count on relatives (primarily male)[11] to help them make decisions and handle their money. For example:

I do call on [my son-in-law] because, well, these investments that I have. Well, it's the economy, and I don't understand them enough to know.... He has helped me a lot businesswise. (Lydia)

Those who have the resources hire professional financial advisors:

Well, I think I've picked up an advisor and an accountant so, "There," I said, "I've got two more husbands," you know, just laughing. (Muriel)

I go to talk to [the advisor at the bank]. I don't know what I'd do without her.... Whereas before um ... if you don't have somebody like that, you don't know whether you're comin' or goin'. (Betty)[12]

Betty depends on her advisor to pay her rent, the telephone bill, the cable television bill, everything "except my clothes and my groceries." She recommends that all widows get a manager like this to handle financial matters. The cost for such a service can be several thousand dollars a year.

Judy reported that she uses a combination of family and a professional advisor. She went to an investment company when RRIFs and GICs came due, but she brought her brother with her to "sit in" and make sure the advisor did not take advantage of her. Judy's need to feel protected is not unusual. Several women reported feeling vulnerable and fearful that someone might try to take advantage of them simply because they are women:

I do feel that sometimes people will try to take advantage of a woman, but not necessarily a widow. It's just because it's a woman, you know. (Polly)[13]

Women's uncertainty regarding money is also evidenced in the barriers to full relationships they have with others because of their feeling of vulnerability in this area. The interviews provide examples of this in terms of relationships with family, friends and others. This is important because we often assume that it is simply the amount of income that matters when it comes to widows and money—some researchers even think that income is more important than emotional loss in determining how well widows adapt to their situation (e.g., Harvey and Bahr 1974, quoted in Martin Matthews 1991, 88)—but it is often the wealthier widows who isolate themselves because of their desire to protect their money.

One of the surprising findings is the problem two of the three widows who had stepchildren and were financially comfortable had regarding financial issues and their relationship with their stepchildren. For example:

> And it was the first thing I realized, the first time I knew something was wrong, when I was reading the will, and I was going slowly and asking if there was anything they wanted me to read over and um ... I read where it said, his RRIF, he left to me, for me, to help me with my, you know, living and um.... And just out somewhere here, I heard, "Yeah, she got the money." (Judy)

Judy went on to explain that when she was moving out of the house (which had been left to her stepchildren as she and her husband had planned), the children showed up. At first, Judy thought they were there to help, but she later realized that they were there to make sure she didn't take anything they felt was theirs. This has coloured her entire experience as a widow—she thought she had a good relationship with her husband's children; now there is practically nothing left of that relationship.[14]

Similarly, Betty, who raised her husband's children, had similar problems regarding family possessions and her decisions to "help" the children when they were in need of funds:

> After he's gone. It was fine before, but of course, we, we were pretty much [financially] ahead of them, and they hadn't got to the place where they felt they were doin' well. And they felt Dad was doing so much better, and they weren't jealous of that. But they had no idea he had saved what he saved, and I, like a big fool, told them.
>
> And they keep sayin', "well, you got mon—" but they read these things ... just after Dad died, and they knew, knew how much money was in there, and it was very little. What's a hundred and ninety-five thousand? It isn't much at all now, and with the rates down, it's not growing.

Betty went on to recount complicated situations of lending or giving money to various children and grandchildren when they needed it. This has complicated the interactions and feelings of Betty and her stepchildren for each other. So, for example, when a grandchild lost a house in a fire, Betty said she would give her some money:

And so I said to them about that, "Well, maybe I could donate five hundred," and "Oh, that's great." So I did the five hundred and ... T. was supposed to give four hundred and B. would make up the [difference]. Come to find out, just talkin' to them ... T. never [gave] anything. Her mother said, "Don't really need it, you need it, don't put anything." And I thought that was kind of underhanded because they waited for me to see what I would offer, if anything ... and that kind of stuck in my craw.

As a result, Betty feels that she has to remain secretive about her financial situation. Now the only person who knows about it is "my girlfriend at the bank."

Muriel has relinquished her relationship with her husband's family and with some friends because of what she perceives as jealousy surrounding the income she has from her husband's having invested his RCMP pension after retiring from that organization while working at another job. She told me the story of a long-time friend who had been with Muriel when her husband died. Muriel thought she was jealous of her ability to "do what I wanted to":

But something happened, and I detected a bit of jealousy.... I bought myself a Christmas present as if it was from him.... And [it] was $375 ... and she said, "If he was living ... you wouldn't have that picture." And I said, "Why?" "'Cause," she said, "he wouldn't have spent that money for it." It sort of hurt me, so it sort of went downhill from there. So I have not seen [her].

Muriel also reports that her sister-in-law had been asking questions about money and she had responded, "That's my business." This has resulted in a virtual severing of that relationship. In fact, when I asked Muriel what she thought is "the most important thing other people should know about being a widow," she told me that you need to

take control of your own life.... There's always someone that you can confide in. And I don't mean the next-door neighbour or like that. Or even your family, if you really, you know, think they might, might not be a safe place to go.... You can go to a lawyer, you know.

Worry about others knowing too much about their financial situation has also led some women to be very cautious about letting acquaintances, business associates or strangers get too close. For example, Eleanor lives in a very small, isolated community and is probably one of the more affluent residents. She is only too aware that others think she is rich and are very curious about her circumstances:

And a lot of it is, they figure that if I can come home and live in this house and drive that car and not have to work, then I've got too much money.

And so I think they see that as a threat.... Anything that I've got since he died, I would gladly give back if I could have him back. But um ... the tombstone that I chose, you know, because it's different, because it's probably bigger. But to me that's nobody's business. But they make it their business anyway.

It bothered me that they started in, you know, "Well, she doesn't need a job. That house is paid for and she got a million dollars when [her husband] died." I'm still waiting for the cheque if I did.

Much of Eleanor's energy is taken up with worrying about the gossip and nosiness she perceives surrounds her position in her small community.

Emily had been in business with her husband, and it was their business associates who seemed to pose the greatest threat to her financial well-being. First, of all:

See, I've often wondered whether if it's because we had a business. People think that all widows are rich.... And so they expect you to pay for everything you have done.... I certainly wouldn't listen to all these guys that said, "Oh, I knew [your husband]; I'll give you a good deal."

According to Emily, these men were actually overcharging her for their service.

Strangers may also represent a danger to a widow when she is considering others' responses to her financial situation. For example, Muriel (who admittedly is more suspicious than others) does not like to tell seat-companions on planes that she is the widow of an RCMP officer, particularly if that seat companion is a businessman:

They always start a conversation, and, of course, they want to know, you know, where you travel, where you work and anything, you know—are you married or divorced. "No, I'm a widow." And, well, "What kind of business was your husband in?" Of course they want to know. I said, "Oh, RCMP." "Oh, you must be financially secure." And I say, "Oh no, I've got a few pensions, that's all." It's not something you go around, you don't go around talking about that.... Sometimes you're tempted to say, "Oh yes, I'm married" ... just to throw them off.

## Concluding Thoughts

Issues surrounding money are not simply a matter of how much income a woman has or if she is poor. Certainly, poverty and/or a significantly lowered income has an impact on the way older women experience widowhood, but their interpretation and others' interpretation of their situation is in some ways even more critical. So women who might, to others, seem to be living in very limited circumstances speak of "making do" and "getting by." These phrases might be used by women in quite a variety of situations.[15] The complexity of the subject is evidenced by the vulnerability and uncertainty these older women felt in the face of red tape, their reliance on others' advice and the secrecy and jealousy surrounding the affairs of those women who appear to have ample resources. This does *not* mean that income does not matter. These women, and older widows, in general, are often forced to live within very limited means after raising families and providing extensive care to their husbands. It does mean that, as with other aspects of their lives, women's experiences are multifaceted and reflect their interpretation.

### Notes

1 Statistics Canada's low-income cut-offs for an unattached individual in 1992 ranged from $15,175 in a city of 500,000 or more to $10,331 in a rural area (National Council on Welfare 1994, 3).

2 Her total annual income is $11,744.

3 The continuing primacy of the symbol of writing a cheque is interesting in light of the fact that, to a large extent, cheques are giving way to ATMs and automatic deposit systems. Of the women who participated in this study, only Lydia spoke of learning to use a bank machine: "I was scared to death of that cash stop thing.... You know, where you go in and get your money out. My daughter ... took me to show me how to do it.... She said, 'Well, I'm very proud of you now.'"

4 In fact, of several textbooks on the sociology of the family I checked, Eichler's (1988) was the only one that even discussed finances.

5 See chapter 2 for a full discussion of the early days of widowhood.

6 Marilyn went on to recount a rather long story about mix-ups and having to go back to an office in downtown Fredericton again and again before they were finally cleared up.

7 And, of course, in New Brunswick, government offices are now closed completely during this holiday period.

8 One would think that with all the computerization of records, a woman could be spared this experience.

9 See van den Hoonaard (1997) for a discussion of this practice's making new widows feel that they no longer exist.

10 Muriel seemed fairly incredulous that private companies would not "take care of their own" the way the RCMP do.

11 Four of my respondents count on sons, a son-in-law or a brother; one counts on her daughter to help with financial affairs.

12 Interestingly, this money manager seems to recommend to Betty that she only worry about herself when she makes her decisions, not her stepchildren. In fact, Betty reports the manager pointed out to her that her husband's grandchildren are not her grandchildren, even though they had been married forty-six years. See March (1995) for a discussion of adoptive children's experiences of not being considered real members of the family.

13 These fears are not unfounded. A financial consultant from a non-profit organization explained to the members of the six-week workshop we ran as part of this study that the lawyers in her town form "a Boys' Club" and some have

been known to impose some very strange charges. The example she gave was a $250 charge for "computer time" that was added onto the usual time charges.

14 Judy also told me that a friend of hers had had a similar experience.

15 See Gubrium (1993) for a discussion of the importance of subjective interpretations of nursing home residents on their evaluation of the quality of care they receive.

# Chapter 8

# Connections to the Community

*T*his chapter looks at women's connections to their community beyond the interpersonal level by looking at a number of different kinds of formal organizations. First it looks at the role of support groups. These groups are not for everybody, and the women in this study report varying levels of involvement, from not being involved at all to having been members of a support group for a number of years.

Next the chapter examines the role of faith and church in the lives of the participants in this study. Again there is a range of importance, ranging from no impact at all to actually providing the organizing rhythm to women's day-to-day lives.

Finally, the chapter looks at involvement in secular organizations. Participation is, once again, characterized by diverse levels of involvement. Some women do not take part in organizations by personal inclination, while others report very full daily involvement. The situation of women in rural communities in which they are relative newcomers is of particular interest because, in communities like these, there may be a principle of seniority (Keith et al. 1994, 60) in which decision-making and positions of importance are reserved for lifelong members of the community.

Notes to chapter 8 are on pp. 133-34.

## The Role of Support Groups

Phyllis Silverman (1986) started one of the earliest support programs for widows in 1967. Her Widow-to-Widow Program involved one-on-one contact between a more experienced and a new widow, as well as some group discussions. Since that time, many programs have come into existence all over North America. There are a variety of models adopted by these programs regarding content and format. Some, like Silverman's Widow-to-Widow Program, match up widows, while others are geared towards specific groups, for example, older widows and widowers rather than widowed persons of all ages. Others cater to younger groups, while still others may be available to members of a particular religion (Prosterman 1996).

Perhaps one of the most important decisions regarding format is whether these groups, workshops or support groups should have a limited duration (a particular number of meetings) or whether they should be ongoing with widows coming in and leaving the group as they feel comfortable. One of the towns in which this study took place does have an ongoing group, which was a little less than five years old at the time of the research. Some of those who participated in this study took part in this group, a couple had participated for a while, while others had not joined at all.[1]

There were a number of reasons for not joining a support group. A widow might not be aware that such a group exists; she might not feel comfortable expressing her emotions in front of others or having others express their emotions to her; she might interpret continuing attendance at a support group as dwelling on her loss and not moving forward; she might object to the idea of participating in activities with a group of widows; or she might think that she simply does not need the help of such a group, that she is independent or self-reliant.

Although a few women do not attend a support group simply because they are unaware that one exists (for example, Doris), most offer a specific reason for not attending one. Several women feel that they would be uncomfortable expressing their emotions in front of others. Lynn, for example, is quite ill at ease even thinking about participating in such a group, and this was very clear in the way she communicated her uneasiness at even imagining herself there:

> I just shied away.... I didn't want to, I mean I can talk to you, but I'm not going to talk to ... it wouldn't help me.

Doris commented that she doesn't "like my emotions showing" and felt that she would be "uncomfortable" in such a setting.

Others feel that they would have to deal with others' emotions at the sessions of such groups and avoid them for that reason. Muriel, for example, reported the experience of a widow she knew to explain why she does "not believe in these sessions":

> I know one girl that went to that and she ended up that everybody was calling her, crying on her shoulder.... I couldn't see getting anything out of that. You're listening to other people's problems.

Some women associate a support group with being "stuck" and not getting on with one's life. Blanche, for example, said that she attended a six-week grief group at the hospital,[2] which had a reunion later on. She did not go to the reunion because "I try to get ahead, out of that, not go back." This attitude is also present in discussions of the ongoing support group for older widows, which appears to some to prevent women's moving forward:

> 'Cause you can only say so much and ... once you have told your story, well then, there is no sense in your repeating it every time. (Florence)

Edith is one person who enjoyed the six-week grief workshop at the hospital, but feels that the ongoing support group is not for her:

> Well, [my son] signed me up for the widow grieving at the hospital.... It was very good. I like that very much, and they started going to one down at the clinic. I went there for a while, but I preferred the one at the hospital because it was only for six weeks, whereas this one, some of them have been going there a year.[3] I don't feel that it's doing them that much good.... I don't think you should keep going back.... Every time a new person came in then they'd go around and tell about how did your husband die and all this sort of thing. After a while it gets a bit, I said to P., "I guess I'm moving on."

Judy simply commented:

> I've cried enough; I don't want to cry any more.

Peg stated categorically that the participants in support groups "do not seem to be making any progress."

In an earlier study of the experience of widowhood in a Florida retirement community (van den Hoonaard 1994), I found that some widows were unwilling to go out with groups of widows. A few women who participated in this study communicated a similar reluctance. Marie, who is in her fifties, for example, felt that she would find "a bunch of old women" in a support group. Peg recoiled from the thought of going on trips with groups made up only of those who were grieving:

> But I don't want to go [on expeditions] in groups with widows. I just want to go in groups.... It sounds [like] the walking wounded.

A sense of self-reliance keeps others from seriously considering attending this type of group. Nancy, for example, seems to feel that those who attend are, perhaps, more needy than she is. In fact, she really couldn't come up with an adjective to describe those who do go:

> They are necessary for those who _____ [voice trailing off].

Others simply feel that they don't need such a group, that they can do it themselves:

> I think I can talk myself into feeling better or worse, either one, either one. (Marie)

> I just figured I don't need it. (Marion)

> I didn't feel I needed it. I had my support. (Sarah)

Sarah, however, articulates her support as being located elsewhere, namely, in her "Three Fs, family, faith and friends," while Eileen wants it from "family and friends" and Lynn had "enough support with my church."

Similar comments explain why some women shy away from reading self-help books related to widowhood and/or grieving. Eleanor commented wryly that

> No, I knew more than they did.... I didn't read any of them.... I think it would have been depressing.

Muriel simply felt that getting through being a widow "is all common sense" while Lynn insists that

> Nobody ever put any rules out on grieving or mourning, so you're really winging it.

Nonetheless, at various places in the interviews many of the participants made reference to stages of widowhood. Marie, for example, became frustrated because she felt trapped in the anger stage, while Audrey worried that she hadn't gone through that stage. Even if one does not subscribe to the idea of specific stages of widowhood, she is likely to know that they exist:

> I played it by ear.... I don't know [about the stages of grief], I don't know any of that. I just had my own stages, I guess. (Sarah)

Four had attended or were attending the ongoing support group for widows. They told me about their experiences in the group and what happens at its meetings. In addition, I was able to attend one regular meeting of the group during which I got a feel for what happens at its meetings.

This group meets once a week, on a weekday morning for an hour and a half in a public meeting room. The ten to twenty women who attend sit in a circle with the facilitator. If there is a new woman at the meeting, the group goes around the circle with each woman's telling a little bit about how her husband died and how long ago. This is followed by either a speaker or a report of how everyone has done during the previous week. There are refreshments, and the participants share news of members who might be ill. During the meeting that I observed, the group gave a gift box full of home-baked items[4] to one of the members who had been ill and was attending her first meeting in a while. In addition to the weekly meeting, the members of the group often take trips together and put on an afternoon tea for "seniors" once a month.

One aspect of the meeting of this group that stands out is that all but one of the women have been attending the group for several years. In fact, only one woman's husband had died within the last two years. She is obviously in a more shaky state than any of the other women and keeps a box of tissues by her side. Although the other members assured her that she is doing very well, it was obvious that most of the women are not grieving as actively as she is.

According to the women who have been active in the group since its beginning, they were all grieving in an active fashion when the group first started. For example, one woman told me that when the group first got started that they would all cry together: "They would sit there with a box of tissues next to each one and cry." Betty, who has been attending the group since the early days, described what it was like when she started attending:

> The first thing they get you to talk about it, and ... it's very hurtful, and there's not been anybody there yet that didn't bawl. And everybody else bawls with them. But it is a very *healing* process. They all have the same beginning, you know, the same feelings, the same agony, the same loneliness. They all have it in common. [Emphasis in original]

This pattern is repeated whenever a new woman attends a meeting. But in recent years, as the majority of women have moved away from intense feelings of grief, the group has expanded its activities and changed the topics of discussion, which now focus more directly on practical concerns such as finances and automobile problems. For example, there was an extended discussion of the challenges of dealing with a hired house painter at the meeting I attended.

The responses of group participants to my queries about the nature of the support group make it clear that participants get something different from the group than they did when it first began. Whereas they tell stories of weeping together during the early days, today they use phrases like:

> It's sort of a get-together, and we talk. (Cathy)

P. said, "Now, in a way, it's almost become a little bit of a social group."
(Marilyn)

But, we're great together. We have a lot of fun and it's really good. (Betty)

Edith, who was a member of the group for a while, noted the transition
that took place after the widows had been together for a while:

> But we used to laugh, and ... we weren't miserable all the time, and they said
> nobody would know this is a widows' group, everybody laughing.

A major addition to the group's activities that has contributed to its
changing nature is their putting on an afternoon tea for

> All people that have no way of gettin' out and gettin' to places.... We cook
> everything and then everybody is looked after.... It takes about an after-
> noon and the cooking that you do beforehand. And it's great for people.
> (Betty)

These teas allow the women in the group to concentrate on something
outside of themselves by offering this service to those who are worse off
than they. At the few teas that I attended, there was no mention of widowhood or any problems the women faced because of their being widows.
On the contrary, the atmosphere was very light with a focus on serving
the "seniors" who were attending:[5]

> So, it's very nice. [The seniors] all enjoy it so much, the people that, a lot of
> them, they can't get out very much.... So it's very nice that they do that,
> really for seniors. (Cathy)

The group also plans and takes trips together. They have gone on
day-long shopping trips to a larger city as well as trips to see the fall
colours and picnics. Betty described one such trip:

> It was only $13 ... and then you bought your own lunch and they dropped
> you off at Eaton's and Simpson's and that gave us a break.

Unfortunately, this activity has been reduced because the bus company,
through which they used to charter a bus, has become less flexible and
does not arrange small tours any more.

It appears that as this group developed over the years, it became difficult to integrate new members. Several people said that new members do
not stay long in the group. Marilyn, who is a member of an ongoing support group dealing with another issue, commented that this is in the
nature of such groups:

> at the [other] group when we went at the first, we were all in the same situ-
> ation. And we progressed, but those that came in after, we weren't in the

same place. Now we could ... give them support and so forth, but they were never the same. New ones need a new group.

In a way, it is the success of the group at helping widows to accustom themselves to their new situation that makes it difficult to integrate new members. They have made friends and enjoy one another. For those I spoke to, it seems that this has become a lively social group in which women have formed strong ties to one another based on having had and communicated to one another "the same feelings, the same agony, the same loneliness" (Betty), sharing practical advice and resources and serving the community.

### The Place of Faith and Church

Involvement in one's church adds another potential connection to the community. It is not, however, simply a matter of belonging or not belonging to a church or attending or not attending worship services. The women who have some involvement in religion described four levels of involvement and meaning. They are: (1) personal faith in God; (2) interaction with the minister or priest of one's church; (3) involvement with the "church family"; and (4) extensive involvement in church activities and/or organizations.[6]

Of the twenty-eight women I interviewed, nine explicitly mentioned that their faith in God is very important to them. Sharon, for example, described faith as "the most valuable thing anyone can have." She credits her not being bitter to her strong faith:

> You have your ups and downs. But I never have any doubts. I have such a strong faith.... I have a lot of faith really, that [I] really don't feel bitter [and] never thought once, well why would He take him and not someone else.

Lynn feels that her faith "helped me more than anything else." While Martha simply commented: "God was my strength."

Belief in God also helps some women to feel that they are not alone: "I just felt that I was not alone" (Martha). Some pray to God in a conversational way:

> I pray myself to sleep every night. God must be getting awful sick of listening to me. "It's me again, God." (Eleanor)

Because many women report that one of the things they miss most about their married life is an interested and caring ear for the small, day-to-day problems and issues that arise in their lives, this habit of "conversation" with God helps to fill that gap. Muriel uses her faith in God to help understand why her husband died when he did:

I have to make my way and accept the fact that it's God's will. I suppose it was.

For several women, their faith in God is associated with belief in an afterlife. This gives them the sense that their husbands still exist and that they will eventually be reunited:

I've been brought up to believe in God and the life hereafter. (Sarah)

It's actually like, with the Christian religion ... its main focus is upon the fact that this isn't the end.... I think it's not your own continuity that you worry about or you feel about; it's the continuity of the other person. You can't think that a beloved person would finish.... It's the sense of the person that you really feel has to go on. (Peg)

I really think he went straight to heaven.... There's no question because he was a good man. (Eileen)

Eileen recounted a story that reinforces her belief that her husband is in heaven:

Two weeks before he died, he called me ... and he said, "Come, Eileen, come." And I said, "Why?" ... And he said, "Look, that door, I can't open that door that's there." I thought it was the morphine talking. So, I said, "Oh, don't worry about the door." I said, "We'll open it some other day." And he said, "No, no, no that door is a special door." And four days before he died he calls me in again and he said to me, "Remember that door I told you a couple of weeks ago? ... Well, it's half open and it has a bright light behind it." And I said, "Does it bother you?" He said, "Oh, no, it's a very peaceful light." He just put his head back and looked up to the ceil ... whatever he was looking at, whatever he was seeing there, and four days later he died. So whether he was getting him ready, the Lord was getting him ready or whatever it is ... the Lord was telling me that the end was coming near.

Eileen was the only person to recount a story like this, and it is obviously a great comfort to her.

Only two women explicitly talked of not having faith. Marie, whose husband died a scant four months before our interview, had this to say:

I go to the Catholic Church, but I lost faith.... Because of this, yes. I think it will come back eventually, but it still is the angry stage.[7]

Lydia, who originally came to Canada as a war bride, credited her lack of a strong faith to her experience in the Second World War:

I think the war changed a lot of people with their beliefs, wondering why.

Nonetheless, she has not completely rejected any belief system. She confides, "I'm religious to the point where I've got to believe in something."

But this is a sharp contrast to those who cannot understand how anyone could survive widowhood without a strong religious faith (for example, Peg).

The next level of involvement, interaction with one's minister or priest, was not mentioned by very many women, but even among the eight women who talked about their experience with a clergy member, the experiences are varied. As early as 1979, Helena Lopata noted the "surprising dramatic failure" (251) of clergy in support systems of widows. Some women do, however, paint a picture of extensive support from their minister, both during their husband's illness and after his death. Martha, in response to my question regarding whether she saw a lot of her minister when her husband was ill, related:

> Oh yes, yes. He was in every day. We have a young minister up here. In fact he was born and brought up [in this village].... He was there, oh, real often.

And, after her husband died:

> The minister, he was [a] great help. He was just a young man, but he's just a sweetheart, you know. He has a very loving way. He visited me quite a bit after [my husband] passed away, but of course not so much now because I'm doing okay, and he needs to visit the ones that need him.

Lydia, who does not have strong religious convictions, was very appreciative of a curate who visited her husband while he was sick:

> She was very good to my husband. She would go in and talk to him ... talk to him and she told me she had really deep talks with him, things that I didn't even know that he would talk about.

This same curate conducted Lydia's husband's funeral.

Cathy did not say very much about faith and does not attend church, nonetheless she has a minister who visits her regularly:

> My minister comes to see me, which is very good.... It's not that I don't want to go [to church]; it's just that I find it hard to go.... But the minister is very good. He comes to see me.... He's good enough to come and visit and have prayers with me, and I appreciate it very much.... [He comes] about once a month ... and especially where I don't go to church, I think it's very decent of him to come.

Cathy attended her church regularly before her husband became ill and she continues to contribute financially. In contrast, Betty paints a different picture of trying to get support from a minister of a church where she was not really known:

> When we came down here, and [my husband] wasn't so well, and our minister changed within a year of the time, and we had a new one, and [my

husband] was getting more sick all the time, and we finally didn't go at all. We lost track of the church and the church never took any interest in us.... And since I don't go to church, nobody comes to get me because I can't get down there.... I think when you get too old, you're not going to be much of a help to the church. You're not needed any more.

Although Betty had asked the minister about openings in a church-run home, "I never heard a word since."[8] Two other women had complaints about their clergy. Edith stated baldly that her minister had visited her only once after her husband died. Marie's situation was a little more complicated. She is a francophone Catholic; her husband was an anglophone Protestant.[9] Although she did receive some support from his church, the francophone priest at her church did nothing. She suspects this is because her husband was an anglophone.

Four women referred specifically to their "church family" or to their Christian friends who were important to them in the days since their husbands died. Doris responded to my question regarding how her life has changed by commenting that not only had her faith increased, but also:

I do find that being Christian helps a tremendous amount because [of] relationships with other Christians.

Peg had more concrete things to say about her "church family," and easily recounted things they have done for her, particularly in the days right after her husband died:

And I found that the church family, when I got back up here [right after her husband died] really enclosed me.... Telephone calls ... they arranged to put on a hot meal for the people who'd come [for the funeral]. This was the church ladies, themselves.... There was all sorts of generous tokens in that way.... So many thoughtful things.

Martha describes the support she receives from her "church family" as ongoing and something that she "couldn't do without." She comments:

They have kept me in prayer.... I've had some of them, very faithful about calling to see how I am making out.... Some of the younger ones have come and told me I was a great inspiration to them.... So, it's just, I just felt that they had been there for me if I needed them.

So, for Martha, it is not simply that people have done things for her, but the security of "knowing they're there." For Sharon, as well, fellow church members were there "a hundred percent."

But friends from church were not available to everyone, and a few women specifically commented that the absence of fellow church members was a disappointment. Cathy, who is not active in her church, feels that this is the explanation for her not receiving support from other members of her congregation. Audrey, on the other hand, is active in her church but found that during her husband's illness, members of her church were there for her:

> During [her husband's illness] I don't know what I would have done without my church family.

After he died things changed:

> Those people just didn't come back after he died.... They came to the funeral.... Now they just are gone. Especially couples in the church.

Audrey's experience reflects the challenges many women mention in their attempts to maintain relationships (see the chapters on Relationships). However, because she associates her disappointment with her church, it may have broader implications in her life.

The two other women who specifically mentioned dissatisfaction with the members of their church live in rural areas in which they did not grow up. For them, being an outsider in the community also extends to their having limited possibilities of connections with other members of their church. Sylvia refers to this as a "lack of togetherness." Florence has strong feelings of rejection associated with her church:

> They're terrible in church.... You can go in and sit right beside them, and they'll talk to the ones next to them.... I feel sometimes as though I'm some kind of outcast or something.

Both Sylvia and Florence have made some attempt to achieve a sense of belonging by joining a church organization. Neither has found her attempt very successful. Sylvia, who depends on others for rides, has tried dropping hints that she'd like to be invited either to a church organization or to be offered a ride to church, but she has found that

> They go every Sunday and they drive, you know, and never really offered me. Maybe I expect too much.

Florence received a call inviting her to join the church choir, which she did, but this has simply reinforced her feeling of exclusion:

> It didn't help in the way I had hoped it would because ... they were clannish and didn't talk to you. And so I didn't get the ... friendship ... that I expected.... I have still been going, but I don't know for how long.

Those who were already active in their church organizations have found that they have continued to provide both fellowship and useful activity. Both Peg and Martha, rural women, are involved in several church organizations that are an integral part of the rhythm of their lives:

> And, of course, [my minister] got me busy on Bible studies and things like that, leadership courses, whatever. I think keeping you busy, but not too busy, is a good idea. (Peg)

> I go twice a week to exercise classes.... That keeps me busy the two nights a week.... We have a nice Bible study now.... I was busy there this morning. (Martha)

Doris, another rural woman, connects friendship with her church activities:

> I found the friends at church and the church activities were worthwhile as well as being something that you spend your time and your interest in church groups. I'm president of the missionary group, and all day Tuesday we work at the church quilting and doing crafts for our craft sale.... Then there's Bible study and I take part in that.

The women who reported that they are active in church groups had been active before their husbands' deaths. Only Lydia stated that she is becoming more involved in her church since her husband's death. She noted that

> I'm trying to do more for the church now because I've never done very much for the church, and I'm beginning to go down and give a hand at the office.... You know they have women go down there, and I'm helping with the altar guild which is something I've never done before.

But Lydia is someone who does have a history of participation in other organizations. In the next section I will look at the participation of these women in organizations that are not affiliated with their church.

### Participation in Secular Organizations

As with any group of women, there is variation in the extent to which they take part in organizations. Some, like Lydia, are heavily involved in organizations and planned activities and cannot really visualize that anyone might not be able to find "something." Blanche, on the other hand, is not a joiner and does little with organizations. Finally, Florence finds herself an outsider in a village—she would like to be active in organizations, but is having trouble breaking in. This section will present the accounts of each of these three women concerning organizations, followed by a discussion of the barriers as well as factors that assist the women to participate in organizations.

Lydia lives in a small city and finds that her time is quite taken up with organizations and activities. She has been a member of two active organizations for many years, and her involvement has continued after her husband's death. It is noteworthy that both of these organizations are women's organizations.

The first organization that Lydia talked about is the Order of the Eastern Star. She had the title of "Worthy Grand Matron," which indicates an intense level of involvement. The members of this group provided much support for Lydia when it was most needed. For example, when I asked Lydia about memories she had from the first few days following her husband's death, she replied:

> I was very fortunate ... my friends [from OES] stayed right with me, like I wasn't alone.... One friend ... knew just what to do and when to do it.... When my husband was sick, she was in here visiting and she brought food in.... My friends got me through that period of time.

When I asked Lydia to tell me more about this organization, she recounted a round of activity and connection that is very strong:

> It's just a wonderful organization.... It's the largest organization that both men and women can belong to in the world.[10] ... In fact I just came from a little craft group ... and we've got a supper coming up.... We cater dinners up in the masonic hall and then we have teas and things.... Monday night I was to M. [a town about an hour's drive away] and there were 120 people there.... Now on Saturday we have a meeting in [a city an hour's drive away].

The Order of the Eastern Star occupies much of Lydia's time. She is also a member of the War Brides, which she describes as a "godsend." There is a wonderful bond among the war brides because they

> are all in the same boat. We're all from England and we can talk about our experiences and what we went through. We have some great jam sessions.... We are all seniors and most of them are widows.

For Lydia, the Order of the Eastern Star and the War Brides provide complementary functions. The War Brides is "more personal" while the Eastern Star is "more spiritual, maybe. It provides for your inner strength."

Certainly, being active in these two organizations would keep many people busy, but Lydia also takes advantage of programs put on by the seniors' section of the Recreation Department of her city. She feels that there are ample activities available:

> But I tell you one thing here in Rivertown the seniors have got it made. You know the widows, there is so much going on in Rivertown. Through the lawn bowling club ... I go on city walks in the mornings.... There is so much going on.

In contrast, Blanche does not avail herself of organized groups, in which she feels she would be uncomfortable:

> I try to go out and meet people, but I do find it very difficult especially if it's a group. I find I can't go for groups ... a large group or a group of strangers.... I just can't go for that.

Blanche does volunteer as a docent at the local Art Gallery, which she enjoys very much, but when I asked her if she has made friendships with other docents that extend outside the gallery she said no.

Blanche spends a lot of time alone, and she attributes that to her not being interested in the organized activities that are available:

> Most of the time I'm on my own. I guess that's probably my own fault that I've never really been a joiner. I don't belong to a lot of clubs and things.... I'm not a bingo player or any of these sorts of things.

Florence, who lives in a small town, would like to be more active in organizations, but finds herself an outsider both because she has recently moved there after living elsewhere for five years and because she has different interests from those who are central in local organizations. Although she describes herself as "not a person who joins," she had been

> secretary of the seniors ... first vice president in the Auxiliary [in the town she lived in until her husband died].[11] helped to look after the canteen for their bingo.... I was the one looked after the visiting of the veterans at the Health Centre in Rivertown up from our Legion.... I was vice-president in the Historical Society up there ... in the choir ... church functions ... and then [when her husband died] I stopped and came down here.

When she moved to her current town, Florence wanted to reproduce that level of involvement, but found that the organizations in that town were not open to her joining in an influential capacity:

> You can't be in the capacity of secretary or president or anything because there's so many people that have to be that and they'll take, you know, they won't let you.

Florence had taken training to be a leader of "High Time," an exercise program for older people that has been very successful and popular in New Brunswick. When she arrived back in H., she suggested that she might put on the program for the seniors:

> And [the president of the Seniors] wouldn't hear tell of it because she didn't know it.... I wanted to have it incorporated in [the Seniors'] meetings, this what they do [in another small town], but this woman wouldn't hear tell of it.

The woman she is referring to acted as a very effective gatekeeper in preventing Florence from interesting other members in the High Time Program:

> One day, I told her, I said, "You know, between the time we have our card games and our supper," I said, "I'm going to go over some of this High Time with the seniors.... There's lots of them that would benefit." So we got there and we're supposed to play ten games.... We got through early this day. And I kept looking at my watch and I thought, "Oh, great, now I'm going to have the time to do this." And just when we were finishing the last game she stood up, she says, "Well, we're gonna have two more games of cards today." So that ended that.

In addition to being an outsider, Florence has different interests from many of the women in her locality and this exacerbates her problem:

> They go and they play cards and eat and go home. That's it, nothing else.... There's so many things that could be done ... to make it more interesting.

Florence recognizes this as an obstacle to her feeling at home:

> Another problem that maybe is my problem ... my interests are different from a lot of people around here ... 'cause I have been a writer and I have written columns in papers.... I wrote a cookbook for the seniors ... I did a directory for seniors ... I wrote a book on medicinal herbs.... I had enough of the ones [where she used to live] that were interested in my interests of family history and medicinal herbs.... When I moved back here they wouldn't hear tell of me doing anything.

Florence most eloquently described the barriers to her being fully involved in organizations. Others also faced a variety of barriers. For example, Emily had been involved in square dancing with her husband. It was that involvement as a couple that led to her discomfort with the organization. She commented:

> I found the hardest thing, and really I find it still hard, to walk into places where there's couples that knew us. Now strangers, it's not a problem. But I still find it difficult to walk into places that, that knew us as a couple.

Sarah also found it difficult to continue volunteering where she had volunteered with her husband, but, unlike Emily, she found that "you get over that."

For Betty and Sylvia transportation constrained their ability to participate in organizations. Peg, who has been very active in civic organizations, said:

> I was involved too much in the reading of the minutes and the gavel and that bit.... I've had enough of it over the years.

As well, she was involved in the setting up of a local museum but remarked, "I know when to back out and leave people alone." Her niece is managing the museum now and "I don't want to go breathe down her neck."

Eleanor is also quite active in civic organizations in her small village. The constraint on the level of her involvement is gossip. Although she is on a number of committees, she does limit what she will do because a man with whom she has a relationship is also on these committees.

The women-only organizations that Lydia talked about make it easy for a widow to continue. Others related additional features that facilitated continuing involvement with organizations. For example, Sharon talked about one of the men who is in Golden Toastmasters with her:

> If we go anywheres like Halifax or things for our Toastmasters, he always makes sure I get a seat, you know what I'm talking about.

And the group in general is "quite a clique, quite close."

Peg's civic group worked together over a long period of time, and therefore its members still get together regularly.

June, whose husband had Alzheimer's disease, continues her commitment to the Alzheimer's Society. In this case, it is her continuing desire to be of service that motivates her activity:

> I still can't get away from helping people with it, you know. I don't go as much ... but all the people that I've had ... in the monthly support meetings ... they still call me and I still call them and we get together.... They just need someone to ... encourage them.

June was so involved with Alzheimer's support groups and the care of her husband that, after he died,

> I didn't know just what to do with myself.... So I just worked with more patients.

Her doctors have urged her to "get out and have a life of your own," but June continues to feel a duty to be of service. At the time of her interview, she was thinking about what new group she could help:

> I'm thinking quite a bit about AIDS, helping with AIDS because I have known a lot of young men, dancers, who have died of AIDS.... On the other hand, I would like to do something with young people, too, because I enjoy children.

June's pattern of service has been set.

At the time of the interviews, three women were in the workforce. However, none of them described relationships with co-workers that extended beyond the working relationship.

Sylvia, who is having trouble connecting with organizations, spoke a lot about the possibility of moving into a seniors' residence run by a service organization. Much of her thought regarding this centred around the need to have activities in which to participate:

> And, of course, at the ... Lodge, they tell me there's bingo and card parties, if you play cards. I don't but ... you walk through the halls and everybody acknowledges everybody else. It's a little community.... There is a community room where they have their bingos and things. And they go away on trips and, well, it sounds exciting in a way.

### Concluding Thoughts

It is clear that there is quite a bit of diversity both in women's level of participation in organizations and in their desire to participate. Simply the desire to participate, however, is not always enough. There is a limited number of types of organizations available. In small towns, they may be limited to church organizations, thus making it more difficult for women who either are not Christian or do not want to be involved in religiously oriented activities. In addition, activities seem to be limited in most places to traditional women's activities like quilting, cards and bingo rather than to more intellectual or traditionally male occupations.

Nonetheless, for the majority of women who participated in this study, the organizational possibilities serve their interests. Particularly the women-only organizations like the War Brides provide a peer group that not only are the women comfortable with but that also has shared many of the life experiences, including widowhood, that they have had. Women who find pleasure in these activities find themselves busy and integrated into their community.

Most strikingly isolated are the two women who are living in very small towns in which they are relative newcomers—in some towns living there only for your adult life can make you a newcomer. These women may suffer from social invisibility or may feel actively ostracized by others who are so comfortable in their lifelong social groups that they do not even notice that there are outsiders living in the community.

### Notes

1 I was able to attend one meeting of this support group. All but one of the ten or so women in attendance had been members of the group for several years.
2 The bereavement group at the local hospital includes anyone who has lost a relative. It is intended to help people within the first few months of their relatives' death when grieving is intense rather than to help them with long-term transitions, as the widows' support group does.
3 In fact, many women have been attending this group for closer to four years since its inception.

4 It is difficult to ascertain how "typical" this meeting was because the facilitator had arranged that my being there became a focus of the group—thus, several women pointed out to me when they were going around the circle that they did not know how they would have survived without the group. These comments may have surfaced without my being there because of the presence of a new member whose husband had died within the last two years, but it is impossible to tell how many comments were made simply for my benefit.

5 One thing that struck me during these afternoons is that, by focusing my relationship with the participants in this research on their experience as widows, I might have lost a sense that their lives *do* entail much more than just grieving. One would never guess that this was a group that was brought together by their shared experience of widowhood simply by attending one of the afternoon teas.

6 This discussion includes only references to Christian and church activities because all the women who participated in this study are Christian. It would, of course, be of enormous interest to look at how women from other religious communities, Jewish, Moslem, Baha'i, etc., talk about the meaning of their beliefs and how their involvement in those groups affects their experiences as widows.

7 Marie wrote to me about a year after our interview. Many things had changed for her over the course of that year, but she did not mention anything about religion or her church in that letter.

8 Betty did receive an invitation and offer of drives from a church of a different denomination from her own, but she commented, "but it's not my church, not the way I want it. So I don't go."

9 In Canada, francophone refers to a person whose first language is French and anglophone refers to a person whose first language in English.

10 In fact, there is a men's and women's branch of the masonic fraternity. A woman has to be affiliated with a Mason in order to join the Order of the Eastern Star.

11 Florence had lived in the small town where she now resides when she was married to her first husband. When she remarried, after he had died, she moved to the town where her second husband lived. After her second husband's death she returned to her first husband's hometown because she owned a house there. She told me that her first husband had not been active in the community (and, therefore, neither had she). This may partially explain her difficulty in trying to break into organizations now.

# Chapter 9

# Conclusion: Discovering New Paths

So, what have the older women who participated in this study taught us about the experience of widowhood? The early part of the study, and of this book, focused on the women as individuals. But as they progressed, the importance of the community context has come to the forefront of the analysis. Therefore, this chapter moves from the individual to the community. For, as C. Wright Mills (1959) taught us, it is the interplay of societal history and personal biography that result in the totality of older women's experiences as widows (Lopata 1996, 211).

### Individuals' Experiences

From the moment women learn their husbands are dying—whether it gives them a long lead time or their husbands die suddenly—they are thrust into a situation with which they are profoundly unfamiliar. Although most women do become widows, an expectable event, they also do not prepare to deal with it. Nonetheless there are cultural and structural expectations that guide and, to some extent, control what they do and how they feel about what they do during this period of their lives.

First of all, during their husbands' illnesses they provide an enormous amount of care-provision that they take so for granted that, although they describe it, they feel no need to explain it. It is simply what they did.

---

Notes to chapter 9 are on pp. 146-47.

Most women attempt to follow their husbands' wishes regarding the extent to which they, together, acknowledge and deal with their husbands' impending deaths. Thus, although culturally we espouse the virtues and benefits of an "open-awareness" dying context (Glaser and Strauss 1965) in which all parties know that the patient is dying and talk about it openly, some women will go along with their husbands' wishes for "mutual pretence" that nothing significant is going on. Or, as at least one widow put it, "where there's life, there's hope" (Lydia). According to her, by accepting the inevitability of impending death, one is giving up.

After their husbands have died, women still try to carry on in accordance with their husbands' wishes. They describe many aspects of their lives in terms of this effort. Thus, they do not want to mourn too much for too long because their husbands would want them to get on with their lives. They often "consult" their husbands in the process of making important decisions and in managing whatever financial resource they have. Their feelings about the possibility of remarriage are at least partially defined in terms of continuing loyalty to their husbands. Widows have "imaginary conversations" with their husbands in which they consult with their "wishes, attitudes, and opinions" in order to makes decisions as well as to contribute to their notions of self (Baker 1991, 540, 545). A few believe they have had some communication from their husbands after they died. Some, like Sharon, find such communication comforting, while Mimi, perhaps reflecting a cultural difference, would recoil from such a communication.[1]

Numbness, shock and a heightened sense of vulnerability characterize the early days after a husband's death. Many report remembering very little from those early days, but the memories of people either being there for them or not remain strong. It is very gratifying if the response is greater than expected or comes from unexpected sources. If the funeral is larger than anticipated or if cards or letters come from surprising people, this indicates a great feeling of warmth from community and friends towards the person who has died and reflects like warm sunshine onto his widow. Conversely, the norm of not leaving a new widow alone can be discovered by hearing the disappointment and hurt expressed by the few women who spent their first night as widows alone.

During this very emotion-laden time, widows also have to begin to deal with the legal ramifications of their husbands' deaths almost immediately. There are many to be informed—Canada Pension, banks, etc.—and they must be informed immediately. The emotional pain of having to show a death certificate and explain one's situation over and over again provides wrenching descriptions and, for some, leads to their "identifying moment" as a widow. This is accompanied by an immediate and irrevocable drop in income, often by as much as 50 percent. Uncertainty about whether or not they will be able to get by on the income they have as well as how to manage and make decisions about that income provides a heightened sense of vulnerability.

There has been some discussion in scholarly literature about whether previous losses make a widow's transition easier or more difficult. O'Bryant and Straw (1991), for example, suggest that coping skills acquired through previous bereavement will assist in a woman's adaptation. Based on the stories told by the participants in this study, I would have to say that it is having experienced life transitions and interpreting them as positive that really makes the difference.

The most striking example of those whose experience with life transitions has prepared them for widowhood (or any transition, for that matter) are the war brides. These women came from Britain to Canada and, if their destination was New Brunswick, moved from places like London to small towns that may not have yet had running water. They left their families in England and learned to deal with in-laws who may have been less than warm and welcoming. These women see widowhood as one more— although the most devastating and challenging—transition they have to deal with. Added to this is the traditional British "stiff-upper-lip" approach, which results in women only allowing themselves a limited amount of time to be overwhelmed by their loss. They believe that, no matter how bad things may get, they should and can always pick up their lives and continue on. Some researchers (for example, Campbell, Swank, and Vincent 1991) identify a personality component they call "hardiness" that allows some women to "resolve" their grief more easily than others. Some cultures, like British culture, seem to be "hardy cultures."

Polly communicated a love of change and a belief in its positive potential. She told a story of her husband's and her immigration to Canada from the United States that reflects her enjoyment in and ability to adapt to situations in which one's feet may not exactly be firmly planted on the ground. She reported that her husband arrived home one day and asked her how she would like to go live in the woods. Within a week, they had sold their car and their house, bought a new car and moved to Maine. After a while they felt they wanted to go into an even more rustic setting. Polly's husband suggested Canada. Polly didn't know anything about Canada at the time except that it was north of the United States. Nonetheless, her husband had read a book on the Miramichi[2] when he was a child and had always wanted to go there. So they bought a British Land Rover and made plans to leave. The day before they left, Polly's husband had gone hunting and got a deer. Polly describes a motley crew of several cars and a Land Rover with a deer and an upside-down canoe on top that pulled up to the border guard. She and her husband had no immigration papers, but they did have all their possessions. In those simpler times, the border guard went in to talk to an immigration officer, and the story ends with Polly and her husband filling out the forms and being let in to Canada on the spot. She recounted a number of such on-the-spur-of-the-moment travelling and risk-taking events that characterized her existence during the life of her marriage. It is not surprising that Polly would embrace transition.

This love of adventure is certainly not the norm, and it would be a mistake to underestimate the tremendous loss suffered by women who are comfortable with life transitions. It does, however, underline the growth involved in overcoming challenges and adapting to change.

### Handling Relationships

Of course these women do not live in isolation, and their relationships change in ways that they did not predict and that made the negotiation very challenging. At the most obvious level, widows experience the loss of some of their friends. This is not a new finding, and there have been many attempts to explain this phenomenon (see Lopata 1996). In the stories the participants told about the loss of friendships we can see that the violation of expectations seems to be one of the primary contributors to this loss. Those expectations may be based on "highly valued, if rarely discussed, norms that have evolved over the course of the relationship" (Rook 1989, 171). This was the case for Eileen who had spent so much time helping a friend in hospital only to discover that this friend was no longer willing to take any part of the initiative required to maintain their friendship, and for Muriel, whose friend overstepped an invisible boundary by criticizing Muriel for spending too much money on a present for herself. Unmet expectations may also be based on what women think their friends should do now that they are widows, as in the case of Emily, who felt that widows should be offered rides by couple friends.

Both in dealings with friends and in dealings with adult children, women report a need to "keep up appearances" and not to appear too needy. With friends, this means that women see the need to keep the depth of emotional suffering to themselves; with children, this means attempting to maintain a balance between what they receive from their children and what they contribute to the relationship.

When women do manage to find this symmetry in their relationships with children and friends, they talk about it with a sense of pride and accomplishment. As sociologist Hazel MacRae points out, the woman who can adapt to this most difficult of life transitions "praise[s] herself and [is] praised by others. To be known by self and others as an independent person [is a] significant and almost essential dimension of the self in later life. 'Independent' [is] a self-reference many [are] proud of" (1990, 261).

Both independence and self-reliance are characteristics that women are pleased to be able to assign to themselves. One way they accomplish this is by making sure they do not impose burdens on their adult children, either emotionally or instrumentally. They conform to cultural norms of being self-sufficient and of both allowing their children to "live their own lives" and of continuing to care for them (Aronson 1990, 71). As Aronson points out, we can see the strength of these prescriptions by looking at the comments of the women who have not succeeded in limiting their own need for emotional support from their children. In Cathy's story, for example, there are numerous references to her feeling that she expects too much from her daughters in combination with her feeling hurt that her daughters seem insensitive to her loneliness. This guilt and shame (Aronson 1990, 76) reflect how deeply the norm of being undemanding is internalized (see also Smith 1991 for a discussion of women's efforts at not interfering in their children's lives and remaining independent).

Feeling comfortable with children who live some distance away seems less complicated. It may be that adult children who live far from their mothers feel less susceptible to their mothers wanting too much from them and becoming a burden, which contributes to stories of flowers and phone calls on difficult anniversaries. Regardless of the reason, however, unless there were already problems with their relationship, as in the case of June, whose son had practically severed his relationship with his parents seemingly because he could not handle the symptoms of his father's Alzheimer's disease, there seem to be few problems with children who have moved far from home. The "intimacy at a distance" (Rosenmayr 1977) that these women are able to maintain with their children seems satisfying and adequate to meet their expectations.[3]

Not surprisingly, women report closer relationships with daughters than with sons. Although both may react to their fathers' deaths by trying to protect their mothers and control their lives, daughters seem more amenable to their mothers' wishes to be treated like competent adults.[4] Perhaps the expectation of closeness results in the extent of disappointment women express when their daughters do not seem to be sympathetic enough, as in Cathy's case, or available enough, as in June's case, when her daughter became involved in a new relationship. When a son is not available enough, it seems easier to blame his wife's demands on his time, as Peg does, while when a daughter is not available enough it is the daughter who seems to be at fault.

Challenges in maintaining relationships with stepchildren provided one of the more surprising findings of this study. There is virtually no research on the connection between widows and stepchildren. There is some evidence that divorce has a negative effect on men's relationships with adult children (Bulcroft and Bulcroft 1991). What is of interest here, however, is the rejection of widows by their husbands' children, even when those children seemed to have a good relationship with the couple during their father's lifetime. This is the case even when their father was widowed rather than divorced, as were Betty's and Judy's husbands, and after many years of marriage. Those whose husbands had been divorced, like Marilyn, may have felt resentment towards their husbands' children, but not the deep rejection felt by Judy and Betty.

Relationships with men provide challenges that are quite different. Some women choose to live in a world of women because they agree, with some researchers, that friendship between a man and a woman is at best difficult and conceivably not even possible (Wright 1991). In either case, the norms of comfortable interaction simply are not there. Some, like Audrey and Marilyn, recount stories that demonstrate the problems in trying to decode approaches from men—is he after a romantic relationship or simply wanting to be a friend?

Changing mores are also an obstacle to continuing relationships with men. Many women assume, rightly or wrongly, that men will want to have sexually intimate relationships with them sooner than they would like. They apologize for their "old-fashioned" ideas, but are not willing to give them up.[5] Uncertainty about the men's attitudes in this area may prevent some from even trying out a romantic relationship.

More basic than fears surrounding changing norms is the desire to remain loyal to one's husband. Women continue to wear their wedding rings for years after their husbands' deaths and persist in identifying strongly as their husbands' wives. Sometimes this strong identification as their husbands' wives extends into continued involvement in his social world (Unruh 1983). Martha, for example, continued her involvement in the Canadian Legion's poppy campaign, associated with Remembrance Day, after her husband's death.

Although only one woman in this study reported that her husband explicitly exacted a promise from her not to remarry (which she did not think was unreasonable), the desire among most women is not to remarry.[6] There are, however, a few, particularly among the younger widows, who stated that they would not be averse to remarriage. They may have to deal with their children's reactions. For example, Eleanor's son reacted strongly when she took off her wedding ring, and he did not want any other man driving his "father's" car. They may also be very aware of and sensitive to the potential for gossip, as both Audrey and Eleanor were.

Women who do want "safe" avenues for non-romantic relationships with men show creativity in finding viable settings. Perhaps it is because, particularly in this generation, many women have reached this point in their lives "without being exposed to real models for non-courting, cross-sex friendships" (Adams 1985, 608). June uses ballroom-dancing clubs for such purposes, while others enjoy getting warm but non-sexual hugs from men out in the open, in front of everybody, at church. Perhaps it is when these safe environments do not seem to exist that women shy away from interacting with men at all.

### Handling New Tasks

Women thus learn new ways of interacting with friends, children and men. They also discover new parts of themselves, partially through learning to do new things. First of all, they learn that they can survive without their husbands. Very significantly, they learn to master tasks they previously felt were beyond them. Some researchers (e.g., Blieszner 1993; Lopata 1979) have suggested that one of the reasons that widows adapt better than widowers is that the new things they must learn to do result in enhancing their self-image. The ability to work small appliances, to hammer a nail and to drive give many women a feeling of satisfaction and of personal growth.

Learning to drive, to take care of and to buy a car transport women into an area where they feel very uncomfortable. Even among younger people, the belief still exists that women might not quite have the ability to drive a car without help.[7] There is a body of folklore and a plethora of jokes that contribute to the stereotype of women being too nervous to handle the decision-making that might be required in a crisis situation while driving, as well as women being incapable of handling the mechanical maintenance of a car (Berger 1986). Many of the women in this study seem to accept the folklore, and even a number of those who know how to drive report discomfort or worry about driving on a highway, in a big city or crossing a bridge.

Another area we often think of as the province of men is that of finance. I was surprised that so many of the women had managed the money in their homes before their husbands' deaths. They, as well as I, had the impression that a lot of older women do not know how to handle money. It is significant that, as cheques and bank tellers disappear, this ignorance is still symbolized by the inability to write a cheque. Only Lydia raised the issue of bank machines. I suspect that if I had thought to ask the question, I would have discovered that most widows are neither familiar nor comfortable with automatic teller machines.

The majority of women were familiar with handling money. Nonetheless, taking full responsibility and making the important decisions regarding their assets was a new experience for them, one that is potentially catastrophic. In this area, as in dealing with possibly unscrupulous salespeople and car mechanics, women feel particularly vulnerable. Those who can afford it rely on financial advisors, sometimes "inherited" from their husbands, to help them make decisions.[8] The prevalence of news coverage that focuses on stock or bond calamities contributes to the feeling of vulnerability on the part of some women.[9]

It is well known that the poorest group in Canada are older widows, and the older they are, the more likely they are to be poor (National Council on Welfare 1990). The myth that women's poverty is caused by their inability to handle money (Lopata 1996) is not only inaccurate but ignores the increased expenses women face when they have to hire people to do some of the tasks their husbands had done. A few women reported that they have taken in boarders to help make up the difference, or at least to help them feel less at risk of not being able to make ends meet, a reminder of times past. Women's acceptance of the myth of inability to handle money in the face of contrasting evidence (Morgan 1986) allows their poverty, at least in part, to stay in the realm of a private problem rather than being seriously dealt with as a public issue that needs to be solved on a societal level (Mills 1959).

Lucille Bearon has written that older women have "no great expectations" for their lives and tend to interpret them as "being as good as possible ... and downplay[ing] the significance of negative [elements in their lives]" (1989, 778). Perhaps that is why they are so consistent in omitting their objective financial status in favour of pointing out that they can survive on what they have. They also take pride in being able to get by on very little, perhaps a carry-over from having survived the Great Depression.

It would be a mistake to underestimate the impact of poverty on the widows who experience it, although they themselves try to minimize its meaning by speaking of "getting by" and "making do." In fact, some researchers have suggested that much of the negative impact of widowhood derives "not from widowhood status, but rather from socioeconomic status" (Harvey and Bahr 1974, 104). Nonetheless, affluence, while obviously preferable to poverty, can impoverish a woman's social life because of her voluntarily keeping others at a social distance in order to avoid jealousy or being taken advantage of by friends and/or family.

### The Importance of Ties to the Community

Women's lives can also be impoverished or enriched by the level of their attachment to their community. Connections to the community contribute to women's ability to deal with the challenges involved with the loss of their husbands. Support groups, especially those that meet for a limited time *and* have a structure that encourages enduring relationships among their members, provide both practical information and, with it, confidence and confidantes. As Lund et al. (1989, 205) reported, self-help groups need to have well-defined objectives to be productive. In smaller cities like Rivertown with a population of about 50,000, it is unlikely that there would be resources for many ongoing groups. Thus, the likelihood of a new widow finding a group to join, should she choose to, is small, unless there is a series of limited-time groups, with new groups starting up every so often. An added benefit to a limited time frame for such groups is the potential for "splinter groups" to develop without worrying about deserting the main group.[10]

Women-only organizations, or organizations that make women feel comfortable when they are not one half of a couple, also provide strands that involve women in their communities. Women are also involved in voluntary organizations and, thus, contribute to their communities in important ways. These organizations also provide potential for making new friends, especially among other widows (Harvey and Bahr 1980, 58).

Churches often continue to be comfortable environments for women who are already known and active members, but do not seem to be as helpful to women who were not involved prior to their husbands' deaths. Lifelong residents in rural areas are able to maintain an active and involved life in their churches. This provides meaning and stability, and, as Bahr and Harvey (1979) found, seems to help them overcome an overriding sense of loneliness.

Research comparing the situation of rural and urban widows has provided mixed results. Martin Matthews (1991) has reported the results of research suggesting that widows have the potential to be quite isolated in rural areas, especially if their children move away; the author's research also suggests that the stability of social networks in small towns may make it easier for widows to maintain friendships. As Fry and Garvin (1987, 32) have pointed out, this type of environment provides "a social field where one is known in his or her entirety as a person and one's social history is known to all."

The flip side of continuity and a place in the community for lifelong rural widows (MacRae 1996) is the social marginality experienced by women who have moved to a rural area late in life. These women seem to be either socially invisible or excluded from active participation. Seniority of leadership and effective gatekeeping can silence a woman who would like to have an influential role. This may also affect women who have not been involved in volunteer organizations earlier in their lives. This may explain Cunningham's 1988 finding (reported in Martin Matthews 1991) that those who remain in a rural area after the deaths of their husbands are typically lifelong residents.

Rural areas and small cities are also less likely to provide a great diversity of activity or organizations. Thus, while Lopata (1988, 117) found that education was the "most important variable influencing a woman's life" in a large city, in all other areas sharing the interests of other age peers may be more important. Those who do not participate in or enjoy the "traditional" pursuits of their age peers in their community may find no activities to their liking and few women to share their interests. This was the case for Florence, who may have enjoyed some prestige as a newspaper columnist and writer at earlier points in her life, but found herself isolated as an older widow in a small town.[11]

Society is providing less and less opportunity for interpersonal interaction on a casual basis. For example, in Rivertown (as, I assume, in many other places), the local coffee and donut shops have replaced counters with tables. As well, the use of ATMs and "super mailboxes" limits occasions for socializing with bank tellers and letter carriers. Super mailboxes have replaced individual mailboxes in rural—and sometimes suburban—areas in order to save money; these large, anonymous mailboxes may be several kilometres from some of the homes they serve. Some widows may find it hard to reach these mailboxes if they do not drive or own a car, and they may also miss daily visits from a letter carrier, who might have been the only person they saw every day. As a result of these changes, organizations in which widows feel comfortable and that provide them with a welcome atmosphere are becoming more and more important. They may be most crucial in rural areas where the elimination of face-to-face services is most pronounced. It is in these very places where those who come from "away" feel most keenly that they are outsiders and those with different interests might find themselves most isolated.

## *Where Do We Go from Here?*

When I first started talking about undertaking this project, a colleague suggested that so many women are now in the labour force that their experiences as widows would not reflect traditional gender issues: after all, they would now have their own income and occupational identity. This study has proved him wrong, at least for this age group. Jane Aronson (1990, 79), who studied retired teachers, specifically chose "a privileged group who had worked outside the home and had a clear occupational identity" for her study of informal care of the elderly. She found that these women, "despite their relative material and social advantages," were experiencing their later years as "precarious and marginal." Thus, it appears that the experience of widowhood will continue to be gendered in significant ways.[12] Some gendered features of the experience disadvantage women—for example, most remain financially disadvantaged. Other aspects—for example, women's ability to care for themselves and to develop friendships—make facets of women's experiences easier.

But what of other changes? How will more general changes at the community and societal levels affect older women's experiences as widows? At this point, we can only speculate.

It is clear that women's relationships with adult children have a significant impact on their experiences and interpretation of widowhood. Societal changes will have an unforeseeable bearing on future experiences. The tremendous growth in divorce rates, lowering rates of marriage and childless or one-child marriages will likely change children's feelings of obligation to their parents, as well as their commitment to family in general. This growth is combined not only with women's increased labour-force participation but also with employers' expectation that women will work long hours, thereby leaving less time than in the past to form close bonds with their children. As well, it means the adult children, female and male, will have less time for their parents.[13]

However, a higher divorce rate also means that more women will have had the experience of adapting from being married to being unmarried previously in their lives. It is impossible to predict how this will affect their experience when they become widowed in later life. It may mean that they already have a group of women friends, whom they have known as single women. Conversely, it may mean that not being in stable couples has lessened the possibility that women will have close, lifelong friends on whom they can depend during difficult periods in their lives.

Increased geographical mobility may mean that a woman's only child lives a great distance away and that friends may have moved away. A secure and reliable social context may be a thing of the past. Or, once again, it may mean that women have improved skills at meeting new people and forging new friendships.

We are living in a time when many of the social supports that we associate with community and citizenship are disappearing. At such times it is the most vulnerable members who will first exhibit the effects of these changes. These more vulnerable members of society are our canaries in the coal mine.[14] It is tempting to identify their experience as a personal problem, located within the individuals themselves. Thus, when we talk of someone as "disadvantaged," we forget that it is the organization of society that makes it inevitable that some portion of that society will be disadvantaged. But we are all affected by the decline of community in ways that may become more obvious as time goes on.

Nonetheless, the abiding impression I have of the women who participated in this study is their creativity, resilience and courage.[15] Although there are many stereotypes about older women as passive and ineffectual (Arber and Ginn 1991), these widows have demonstrated great strength, determination and success in their efforts to confront the most profound transition of their lives.

### Notes

1 Parkes (1988) reports that 50 percent of widows say they have felt the presence of a dead partner.

2 The Miramichi is an area of New Brunswick that is known for salmon fishing, hunting and beautiful scenery.

3 We should not forget, however, that most of these women also have at least one adult child who does live within driving distance.

4 See Hansson and Remondet (1988) for a discussion of the challenges older widows sometimes have in trying to maintain personal control and independence in their relationships with their children, particularly sons.

5 See Esposito (1987) for a discussion of the error of assuming that "old-fashioned" ideas are inferior to up-to-date ideas, and how this error leads to cultural stereotyping of older people.

6 A number of women report that their names are already engraved on joint tombstones with their husbands, indicating their expectation to remain single.

7 It is still a common experience, for example, for a man who happens to be walking by a woman pulling out of a tight parking spot to, spontaneously and unasked, start directing her. He must assume that she is incapable of manoeuvring out of tight spots on her own.

8 The difference in experience reported by widows of RCMP officers, who are "taken care of" by an RCMP advisor who helps them through the bureaucratic nightmare they face, is very telling.

9 The media and the police encourage a general fear of crime in this group, which may or may not be warranted. For example, one woman told me that a friend of hers had been advised to look underneath her car in a parking lot at night before getting into it. In addition, a local police department hands out a

pamphlet entitled "Woman Alone," which not only gives hints about how to protect oneself but also heightens one's sense of being a potential victim.

10 For example, two women in the "Striving on Your Own" workshop became close friends and even took a trip to a sunbelt state together.

11 Previously, educated women might have decided to take university classes. However, in recent years universities in New Brunswick have decided they can no longer afford to allow "seniors" to attend without paying tuition. This may result in widows no longer being able to afford to take courses, especially considering that most have experienced a 50 percent or more drop in income with the death of their husbands.

12 Because of the gendered nature of widowhood, research from a feminist standpoint would add a critical component that I have not included because of my desire to present the women's lives as *they* understand them. I look forward to seeing such an approach in research on women's experiences of widowhood.

13 See Hochschild's *The Second Shift* (1989) and *The Time Bind* (1997) for an insightful discussion about children paying the price for the family taking a back seat to paid employment.

14 Coal miners used to take canaries into the mines with them. If the canaries died, they knew there was a methane gas problem and that it was time to leave the mine. Unfortunately, we do not find it so easy to leave and find a better society.

15 Lopata (1996, 221-22) comments that this is a consistent finding in contemporary research on women's dealing with widowhood.

# Part Four

## Appendices, Bibliography and Index

# Appendix A

# *Methodology*

*T*he purpose of this study was to discover the social meaning of widowhood from the perspective of the women who have experienced it. I therefore designed it to highlight the issues each woman feels are central to her experience. There were three parts to the study: *in-depth, narrative interviews*—with twenty-seven women ranging in ages from fifty-three to eighty-seven, with an average age of sixty-five, half residing in urban and half in rural areas of New Brunswick;[1] *observation of a support group*—a six-week workshop, "Striving on Your Own"; and *a focus group*—during the last week of February 1997, a group of ten women met to discuss the findings of the project which had been circulated in a ten-page summary to each woman.

### The Interviews

In the initial planning stages, I knew two basic things that I wanted to accomplish in the process of doing the interviews. The first was to interview a group of women over fifty who had experienced widowhood within the previous five years and who lived in a variety of areas of New Brunswick. Second, I wanted to avoid the compartmentalization of experience that is characteristic of much research and that is "incongruent with women's experiences" (Devault 1990, 96).

---

Notes to Appendix A are on pp. 160-61.

The first step in finding participants for the research was to contact the local newspaper in Rivertown and to request that one of the reporters do a story on the proposed research. The response to the article indicated that many widows appreciated the opportunity to tell their story to someone who was actually interested in hearing it. By nine o'clock the morning after the story appeared in the newspaper, I had received five phone calls from women who were interested in being interviewed. Within the next week I had received over twenty phone calls.[2] The other eight participants were located through a combination of publicity in specialized publications such as the *Third Age Centre Newsletter*, an internal newsletter of New Brunswick's Extra-Mural Hospital, and *The New Clarion*, a bi-monthly newspaper for seniors that is distributed provincially and through personal referral.[3]

Confidentiality of the participants in this type of study is always of paramount importance. In order to protect the women's identities, I have changed their and their husbands' names. In addition, I have altered some details of their stories and of the descriptions of the places in which they live in order to prevent individual identification.

I interviewed all of the women in their homes, at times convenient to them, using a very open interview schedule that would encourage them to tell their own story in their own way.[4] I taped all the interviews with the permission of the participants and each was transcribed in full.

The women came into the interviews with a variety of expectations about what the interview would be like. Some had prepared tea or, in two cases, invited me to lunch. This effort to interpret our roles as ones of host and guest helped establish a relaxed, intimate atmosphere.[5] Others seemed nervous at the beginning and demonstrated their uncertainty by making comments like: *I hope this is what you're looking for.* One woman had a written statement prepared so that she would not forget anything she wanted to tell me.

Regardless of how the interview started, the women visibly relaxed as the interview progressed and they told their story. Several of those who appeared nervous at the beginning of the interview at some point seemed to become aware of the host-guest potential of our encounter and suddenly offered me coffee or tea, which I always accepted. Most of the women showed little interest in hearing about me, but a few did insert comments about books or current events into the conversation in an attempt to normalize it.

The interviews ranged in duration from about one and a half hours to five hours, with the average lasting about two hours. Some women showed strong emotions from time to time during the interview, but none declined to discuss an issue because it was too difficult. At the end of the interview a number of the women thanked me for the opportunity to tell their story and commented that they had told me things they had never shared with anyone else. I seem to have provided them with both a listener and a stranger who, as Simmel (1971, 145) wrote, "receives ... confidences" and then "moves on."

### "Striving on Your Own"

In the initial planning of this study, I anticipated observing a support group for older widows that takes place in a small city in New Brunswick. The support group meets weekly and I hoped to attend meetings for about a year to see how such a group functions and the role it plays in older women's transition to widowhood. It did not occur to me that the members of the group might not welcome my presence.

When I called the facilitator of the group, she seemed quite reluctant to have me come, but did agree to bring my request to the group. She later reported that the members of her group had indicated that having a woman there who was not a widow might make them feel self-conscious. The leader did, however, tell me that I was welcome to come to one meeting of the group.

During the one meeting of the support group that I was permitted to attend, I learned that this group puts on a tea for seniors at a local church hall once a month. I was able to get permission to help serve tea. Because the group was so reluctant to let me observe their meetings, I refrained from taking field notes at these teas.

I was taken completely by surprise several months later when the leader told me that some members of the group had read an article I had written for *The New Clarion*, a provincial newspaper for seniors, on the subject of widowhood. She reported that they had felt "exposed," that I had written about things I had heard from them. Although I assured the leader of the group that I had not taken field notes and that the women recognized themselves because some of the experiences are so common, she insisted that I was no longer welcome at the teas.[6]

This expulsion from the weekly support group led to the planning and holding of "Striving on Your Own," a six-week workshop designed and carried out in partnership with the Third Age Centre. This workshop focused on practical rather than emotional issues, although the participants did bring up emotional issues from time to time. The participants were recruited through publicity and all knew that it was part of a research project and that I would be attending and taking field notes.

The group was organized and led by the director of the Third Age Centre. This partnership was very productive because the Third Age

Centre has expertise in group process while I was able to suggest topics of discussion that would be particularly salient for older widows, based on what I was learning from the in-depth interviews. Some topics were added at the request of members of the group.

There were nine widows who participated in the workshop, including two who acted as facilitators during the session, as well as three staff members of the Third Age Centre. Each session started with the women meeting in smaller groups to discuss how their week had been and any-thing in particular they wanted to tell the group. We then came together for a half-hour presentation on the topic of the week. This was followed by a refreshment break and small-group discussions. Finally, the whole group came together at the end of the morning to hear the results of the small-group discussions. Weekly topics included the challenges for chang-ing relationships, financial planning and the myths of widowhood.

By the third week, the group had become quite cohesive and dis-cussed issues that transcended those that were formally presented. At the end of the six weeks, the participants felt that the experience had been a good one and indicated a desire to continue meeting on their own. Several of the women had made important decisions during the six weeks and a few had made close personal friendships that continue as of this writing.

The findings from "Striving on Your Own" complement those that resulted from the interviews and, in some cases, highlighted the gendered nature of widowhood even more clearly. For example, the participants ini-tiated an extended discussion of the difficulties of hiring repairmen and the vulnerability they felt in this area as single women. Although this issue did come up in the interviews, listening to the way the participants in the workshop shared stories among themselves shed a bright spotlight on this and other challenges.

### The Focus Group

On a sunny day in February 1997, ten women met around a table in a Chi-nese restaurant to discuss the findings of this study. Six of the women were widows who had participated in the study in some way, either as interview subjects or as participants in "Striving on Your Own." One woman was a widow who had not previously participated in the study, but had been invited by one of the other participants. The others were myself and members of the Third Age Centre. All the people at lunch that day had read a ten-page summary of the findings of the study and came with both their appetites and their opinions.

After lunch I turned on the tape recorder, and we began to discuss the summary I had circulated. For the most part, the women said that they felt the findings rang true for them. No one questioned their correctness. Nonetheless, several women, rather than suggest that I might have interpreted something incorrectly, felt moved to criticize some actions of other widows. One felt that some of the women must have had less education than she, while another noted that a woman's pleasure in having a prominent person attend her husband's funeral was inappropriate.

I had hoped that the focus group would generate more data than it did. Those who had been participants in "Striving on Your Own" concentrated on the positive experience the group had been for them. Nothing untoward jumped out of the findings in the opinion of the women who came to lunch that day, and the women's comments did confirm the overall tone of the findings of this study.

### *The Sample*

The women who participated in this study live scattered around the province of New Brunswick. Half live in rural areas and half in urban areas. Thirteen were born in New Brunswick, three were war brides who immigrated to Canada just after the Second World War, three were born in the United States and one hails from Quebec.

All but two of the participants are anglophone. One participant is a francophone from Quebec who lived in a small town in New Brunswick with her English husband for many years. When he died, some friends asked her if she had plans to move back to Quebec, but she was insistent that New Brunswick is her home. One of the war brides reported a similar experience.

The other participant is a Native woman who has lived on the same reserve in New Brunswick all her life. She is a well-known, award-winning craftsperson, living in poverty, who has been generous in sharing her life experiences with many non-Native individuals. As a result, I learned a great deal about the challenges of growing up Native in New Brunswick, including her having to take grade eight classes for three years in a row because the local priest did not give her permission to go into the closest city to a non-Native school while she was required by law to stay in school.[7]

The widows ranged in age from fifty-three to eighty-seven with an average age of sixty-five. They had been married an average of thirty-five years, with the length of marriage ranging from five to fifty years. Fifteen of the women had been married for more than forty years. Four women were widowed from a second marriage—two had been divorced and two widowed. Seven women had been married to men who had been married before—three had been previously divorced and four previously widowed.

Only two of the participants did not have children of their own, and both had been married to men who had children from a previous marriage. Most of the women reported having at least one child who lived locally. Only one woman reported having none of her children living within two hours' driving distance.[8]

Many of the women had been in the labour force sporadically. Seven had either worked before marriage, between two marriages or off and on during their marriage in clerical occupations. Five of the women reported that they had stayed home to raise their children and take care of their husbands during the life of their marriage. Three participants had been teachers and three others had had professional careers. One woman wrote newspaper columns and books on medicinal herbs and family history and was still sought after as a speaker on these topics. Four women were still in the labour force at the time of their interview: one was a nurse, two were part-time university professors and one a professional librarian.

Although a few of the participants' husbands were professionals—for example, a doctor and two accountants—the husbands, in general, reflected a wide variety of occupations, including railroad worker, machinist, dairy farmer, civil servant and small-business owner.

The following few pages contain profiles of each of the women who participated in the study. The names are all fictitious. As well, some details have been changed in order to protect the confidentiality of these widows who shared their stories with me.

### Profiles of Participants

**Peg** is a woman in her late sixties who lives in a small town in central New Brunswick. A war bride, she was born in the United Kingdom and was married to a native New Brunswicker for close to fifty years. She had been a secretary before moving to Canada, and was very involved in civic work with her husband, who was a forest ranger. She has one daughter and one son. Both live about one hour away. Peg is active in her church and is a great reader.

**Edith** is in her early seventies and is also a war bride who was married for almost fifty years. She lives in Rivertown and has four sons, all of whom live close by. Edith worked in an office and her husband worked in a garage.

**Florence** is a seventy-year-old woman who lives in a small town. She has been widowed twice. Florence's first husband was a schoolteacher and her second, to whom she was married for five years, had retired from working for the railroad. Florence has two sons who live locally. She has written books on alternative medicine and genealogy.

**June** is in her early seventies. She was born in the United Kingdom and attended college for one year. June, a war bride, worked as a secretary during the Second World War. Her husband of forty-five years had been an officer in the military and had worked as a personnel director. June's husband had Alzheimer's disease, and she was instrumental in organizing her local Alzheimer's Society. She has one daughter who lives locally and a son who lives out West. June spends her winters in a sunbelt state.

**Polly** is in her mid-sixties and lives on the outskirts of a city. She and her husband of almost thirty years had both been previously divorced and each brought three sons to their marriage. Polly attended a trade high school where she trained as a seamstress. She worked as a dressmaker between her marriages. Polly's husband was a machinist. Born in the United States, she and her husband moved to the Maritimes on a whim, and she has lived here ever since. She has an excellent relationship with her six sons and lives in an apartment over the detached garage of one of her sons.

**Audrey**, in her mid-fifties, hails from Central Canada and lives in a city. She was married for thirty years to a man who worked for the government. Audrey has had a consulting business and has taught part-time at a local university. She has two daughters, one of whom lives locally and the other overseas.

**Lydia**, a war bride, is close to seventy years old and lives in Rivertown. She has secretarial training and has worked in a bank. Her husband was an accountant, and they were married for some fifty years. Lydia is very active in community organizations. She has two daughters. One daughter lives outside of town and suffers from a chronic illness; her other daughter lives in another province in Eastern Canada.

**Eileen** was born in a large American city and lived in Rivertown when we met. She was married for some forty years and taught a language class at a local university. She stayed home with her children when they were growing up while her husband worked for a public company at a professional level. Eileen has two daughters, one of whom lives in Central Canada. She has recently moved into a wing of her other daughter's house in a town outside of Rivertown.

**Mimi** is the only Aboriginal woman who participated in this study. She has a grade eight education because, when she was a child, the priest on her reserve allowed only a few children to go into town to continue their education. Mimi is an accomplished craftsperson and previously owned a shop. She has nine living children, most of whom live locally and two of whom live with her. Mimi is seventy years old and was married almost forty-five years to a man who worked as a foreman in highway construction.

**Emily** lives outside of Rivertown where she and her husband of forty years owned an automotive business. She is sixty-five years old and has training as a bookkeeper. Although she has given up the automotive company, she now has a distribution business. Emily was born in the United States, but moved to New Brunswick when she was a small child. She has three sons and one daughter. Two of her children live out-of-province, one lives locally and one lives with Emily.

**Eleanor**, a woman in her fifties, lives in an isolated town in New Brunswick where she was born. She has done accounting work, and her husband of almost thirty-five years worked for a public company at a professional level. Eleanor's father lives in a local nursing home, and her mother-in-law also lives in the same town. Both Eleanor and her husband were active in civic affairs and local politics. She has two sons, one of whom lives out-of-province. The other son lives in a city about two hours' drive away.

**Judy** is in her early seventies. She has been married twice, as was her husband of ten years. Judy lives in the same city as her son. Judy's husband has adult children, but they have had very little contact since he died. Judy was in the labour force between her two marriages. She was born in New Brunswick.

**Sarah** is in her late sixties and was born in the New Brunswick city in which she lives. She was married for forty-five years to a man who was a welding inspector. She was a teacher prior to retiring and currently winters in the southern United States. Sarah is very involved in her church and has one son and one daughter, both of whom live within an hour's drive away.

**Muriel** was born in a Maritime province and has lived in Rivertown for twenty-one years. She is just over sixty years old and was married for thirty-five years to a policeman. She has two children, one of whom lives about two hours away by car. The other child lives out West. Muriel was only in the labour force for a few years, when she sold handmade items.

**Martha** lives in a small town and is in her early seventies. She was married for close to fifty years to a man who owned a freight-hauling business for many years. Martha worked as a waitress before her marriage and did some bookkeeping for her husband's business. Martha's mother lives in a small town nearby. She has four daughters. Two live in the same town as Martha and two in a nearby city.

**Sylvia** comes from a large American city and lives in a small town in New Brunswick. She was married twice, once to a military man and more recently for sixteen years to a farmer. Sylvia worked as a secretary and store clerk before and between her two marriages. She was not in the labour force while married. Sylvia has three children who all live out-of-province although she does have some grandchildren who live in New Brunswick. Sylvia is about seventy years old.

**Lynn** lives in Rivertown and was married only once. She has a child who lives out-of-province and one who lives nearby. Lynn's husband went to university as an adult. Lynn did not participate in the labour force during her marriage; rather, she stayed home with her children.

**Nancy** is about seventy and was married for forty years. She was born in the province and worked as a teacher. Nancy's husband was a forest ranger. She has three daughters and one son. One of her daughters lives in Western Canada, and her son lives close by. After her husband died, Nancy moved to Rivertown to live near a sibling.

**Marion** is in her late fifties. Born in the United Kingdom, she came to Canada as an infant. Marion has a graduate degree and works in a professional field. She was married for twenty-eight years to a professor who was about twenty years older than she and who was retired for most of their marriage. Marion has one stepdaughter who lives out-of-province, as does her mother.

**Cathy** is close to eighty years old and was born in New Brunswick. She was married for forty-seven years to a policeman who worked for a paper company after retiring from the police force. Cathy had a tea room before she met her husband and worked as a clerk for a while. She also volunteered at a local hospital. Cathy has two daughters, one who lives in the same building in Rivertown as she does and one who lives several hours' drive away.

**Sharon** is in her mid-sixties and was married for some forty-five years. She was born and grew up in a small town in New Brunswick and currently lives in Rivertown. Sharon's husband worked as a supervisor in a construction company. She had a grade ten education, but got her high school diploma in middle age. Sharon did not participate in the labour force. She has four sons who all live nearby.

**Marilyn** is in her early sixties. She was married for sixteen years. Marilyn's husband had been divorced, but this was her only marriage. She worked as a flight attendant and as support staff in a university before her marriage, but did not participate in the labour force after marrying. Marilyn's husband did building maintenance. Marilyn lives on the outskirts of Rivertown. She has no children of her own and is not close to her husband's children.

**Betty** is in her mid-eighties and was married for over forty-five years. Her husband had been widowed prior to their marriage. She has two stepsons and one son of her own. Betty attended business college and worked in a department store as a clerk before her marriage. She was born in New Brunswick and lives in Rivertown.

**Frances** was eighty-seven years old when I met her. She had had a long-term marriage and lived in an apartment in Rivertown to which she and her husband had moved when he began to have health problems. Prior to that they had lived in a rural area. Frances's husband was a farmer. She has one daughter who lives out West, but is close to a niece who lives nearby.

**Doris** is in her late sixties and lives in the small town where she was born, about a half hour's drive away from a city. She has a graduate degree and worked as a teacher prior to retirement. Doris's husband of almost forty-five years taught at a community college. They have two sons and one daughter, all of whom live within close driving distance, although not in the same village as their mother. Doris sees at least one of her children every weekend.

**Blanche**, in her mid-seventies, was born in the United Kingdom but was not a war bride. Her husband of fifty years was a doctor, and they lived in Rivertown. Blanche has six children who all live *scattered around*. Several live within a few hours drive of their mother and the others live out-of-province. Blanche has worked in a nursery school and selling jewellery for a while. She volunteers in a local art gallery.

**Marie**, a francophone in her mid-fifties, lives in a small town in central New Brunswick. She and her husband, a bank manager, were married for nineteen years. Marie is a registered nurse who was working part-time when I interviewed her. She has parents living nearby and a daughter who attends university several hours away.

### Notes

1 In a predominately rural province like New Brunswick the distinction between rural and urban areas can be difficult to ascertain. I defined a rural area as any area where there was no public transportation available.

2 These calls included one from a woman who had been a widow for over forty years! I was quite intrigued that her feelings about being a widow are still vivid and important enough to prompt her to volunteer. Since that time several "lifelong" widows have commented that they would have liked to participate in the research, and one of the widowed facilitators of the workshop that took place as part of the research had been a widow for at least thirty years. This group of women, who have spent most of their adult lives as widows, would provide a very interesting subject of study.

3 This is obviously not a representative sample. Nonetheless, the widows do describe a variety of experience and a depth of experience from which we can gain a great deal. Studies including women whose marriages were more challenging as well as studies with greater cultural diversity still need to be done.

4 See Appendix B for a copy of the initial interview schedule.

5 See Oakley (1981) for a discussion of the special challenges of women interviewing women.

6 A few months later I ran into one of the participants who asked when I would be coming to help with the teas again and told me that I was missed. I told her what the leader of the group had told me and she seemed amazed. I can only conclude that the leader of the support group, as gatekeeper, had her own reasons for not wanting me to attend group gatherings.

7 Both the cultural differences and the experience of growing up as a member of a group that has been so severely discriminated against combine to result in an experience of widowhood that is quite distinct from that of the other women who participated in this study. We know very little of how being Native affects the experience of aging, in general, and of widowhood, in particular. These are studies that need to be done.

8 This is consistent for older Canadians, in general. In 1990, approximately 72 percent of women over sixty-five reported that the child they had the most contact with lived within fifty kilometres (Elliot 1996, 36-37).

# Appendix B

# Interview Guide

1. Where and when were you born?
2. How long were you married?
3. What I'd like for you to do now is tell me about your experience with being a widow. You can begin wherever you like, and include or leave out whatever you choose. I'm just interested in finding out about your experience. Could you tell me about this?
4. What are your most vivid memories from the first few days after your husband died?
5. How would you say your life has changed since your husband died?
6. What has been the most difficult aspect of your life since his death?
7. Anything that particularly surprised you?
8. Have you ever lived alone before?
9. Has your relationship with your children changed since your husband died? How? Friends?
10. Do you remember the first time you thought of yourself as a widow?
11. What are the most important things other people should know about the experience of being a widow?
12. How would you say you have changed since your husband died?
13. Money
14. Decisions
15. Relations with men—wedding rings
16. Weekends; difficult times
17. Mothers as widows?
18. Church support?
19. Is there anything that I haven't asked you about that I should have?

# Bibliography

Adams, R. G. 1985. "People would Talk: Normative Barriers to Cross-Sex Friendship for Elderly Women." *The Gerontologist* 25(6): 605-11.

Allan, G. A. 1979. *A Sociology of Friendship and Kinship*. London: George Allen and Unwin.

Arber, S., and J. Ginn. 1991. *Gender and Later Life: A Sociological Analysis of Resources and Constraints*. London: Sage.

Aronson, J. 1990. "Women's Perspectives on Informal Care of the Elderly: Public Ideology and Personal Experience of Giving and Receiving Care." *Ageing and Society* 10: 61-84.

Averill, J. R., and E. P. Nunley. 1988. "Grief as an Emotion and as a Disease: A Social Constructionist Perspective" *Journal of Social Issues* 44(3): 79-95.

Bahr, H. M., and C. D. Harvey. 1979. "Correlates of Loneliness among Widows Bereaved in a Mining Disaster." *Psychological Reports* 44: 367-85.

Baker, P. 1991. "Socialization after Death: The Might of the Living Dead. Pp. 539-51 in *Growing Old in America*, 4th ed., ed. B. B. Hess and E. Markson. New York: Transaction Books.

Bearon, L. B. 1989. "No Great Expectations: The Underpinnings of Life Satisfaction for Older Women." *The Gerontologist* 29 (6): 772-78.

Becker, H. S. 1970. *Sociological Work: Method and Substance*. Chicago: Aldine.

———. 1996. "The Epistemology of Qualitative Research." Pp. 53-71 in *Essays on Ethnography and Human Development*, ed. R. Jessor, A. Colby and R. Schweder. Chicago: University of Chicago Press.

————. 1998. *Tricks of the Trade: How to Think about Your Research while You're Doing It*. Chicago: University of Chicago Press.

Berardo, F. M. 1970. "Survivorship and Social Isolation: The Case of the Aged Widower." *The Family Coordinator* 19: 11-15.

Berger, M. L. 1986. "Women Drivers: The Emergence of Folklore and Stereotypic Opinions Concerning Feminine Automotive Behavior." *Women's Studies International Forum* 9(3): 257-63.

Bertaux, D. 1981. "From the Life-History Approach to the Transformation of Sociological Practice." Pp. 29-45 in *Biography and Society: The Life History Approach in the Social Sciences*, ed. Daniel Bertaux. Beverly Hills, CA: Sage.

Blau, Z. S. 1973. *Old Age in a Changing Society*. New York: Viewpoints.

Blieszner, R. 1993. "A Socialist-Feminist Perspective on Widowhood." *Journal of Aging Studies* 7(2): 71-82.

Brothers, J. 1990. *Widowed*. New York: Simon and Schuster.

Bulcroft, K. A., and Bulcroft, R. A. 1991. "The Timing of Divorce: Effects on Parent-Child Relationships in Later Life." *Research on Aging* 13(2): 226-43.

Caine, L. 1974. *Widow*. New York: William Morrow.

Campbell, J., P. Swank and K. Vincent. 1991. "The Role of Hardiness in the Resolution of Grief." *Omega* 23(1): 53-65.

Charmaz, K. 1980. *The Social Reality of Death: Death in Contemporary America*. Reading, MA: Addison-Wesley.

————. 1991. *Good Days, Bad Days: The Self in Chronic Illness and Time*. New Brunswick, NJ: Rutgers University Press.

Cohen, L. 1984. *Small Expectations: Society's Betrayal of Older Women*. Toronto: McClelland and Stewart.

Cunningham, G. E. 1988. "Health Status and Coping among Elderly Rural Widows: Residential Differences." Unpublished M.H.S. thesis, Faculty of Health Sciences, McMaster University, Hamilton, ON.

Davidson, K. 1995. "How Older Men and Women Reconstitute their Lives after Widowhood." *Ageing in a Changing Europe: Choices and Limitations*. III European Congress of Gerontology, 30 August-5 September.

Devault, M. 1990. "Talking and Listening from Women's Standpoint: Feminist Strategies for Interviewing and Analysis." *Social Problems* 37(1): 96-116.

DiGiulio, R. 1989. *Beyond Widowhood: From Bereavement to Emergence and Hope*. New York: Free Press.

Dohaney, M. T. 1989. *When Things Get Back to Normal*. Porters Lake, NS: Pottersfield Press.

Doyle, V., with B. Backman, E. Cassiday, B. Cumby, B. Ferneyhouch, J. Florczyk, W. Gladman, P. Hall, P. Joyce, A. MacLean, M. Miller, P. Rafferty, R. Riley, D. Ritchie, J. Smith, D. Trohan and V. Ward. 1994. *It's My Turn Now: The Choice of Older Women to Live Alone.* Gerontology Research Centre, Simon Fraser University at Harbour Centre.

Edwards, M. 1981. *Financial Arrangements within Families.* A research report of the National Women's Advisory Council, Canberra.

Eichler, M. 1988. *Families in Canada Today: Recent Changes and Their Policy Consequences.* Toronto: Gage Educational Publishing.

Elliot, G. 1996. *Facts on Aging in Canada.* Compiled by The Office of Gerontological Studies, McMaster University, Hamilton, ON.

Esposito, J. 1987. *The Obsolete Self: Philosophical Dimensions of Aging.* Berkeley, CA: University of California Press.

Faraday, A., and K. Plummer. 1970. "Doing life histories." *Sociological Review* 27(4): 773-98.

Fengler, A.P., N. Danigelis and V. C. Little. 1983. "Late Life Satisfaction and Household Structure: Living with Others and Living Alone." *Ageing and Society* 3: 357-77.

Festinger, L. 1962. *A Theory of Cognitive Dissonance.* Stanford, CA: Stanford University Press.

Fine, G. A. 1990. "Symbolic Interactionism in the Post-Blumerian Age." Pp. 117-57 in *Frontiers of Social Theory: The New Synthesis*, ed. G. Ritzer. New York: Columbia University Press.

Fletcher. S., and L. O. Stone. 1980. "The Living Arrangements of Older Women." *Essence: Issues in the Study of Ageing, Dying and Death* 4(3): 115-33.

Fry, C. L., and L. Garvin. 1987. "American After Lives: Widowhood in Community Context." Pp. 32-47 in *Widows*, vol. 2 of *North America*, ed. H. Z. Lopata. Durham, NC: Duke University Press.

Glaser, B. G., and A. Strauss. 1965. *Awareness of Dying Contexts.* Chicago: Aldine.

Gorer, G. 1965. *Death, Grief, and Mourning in Contemporary Britain.* London: The Cresset Press.

Gubrium, J. 1993. *Speaking of Life: Horizons of Meaning for Nursing Home Residents.* New York: Aldine de Gruyter.

Haas-Hawkings, G. S., M. Ziegler Sangster and D. Reid. 1985. "A Study of Relatively Immediate Adjustment to Widowhood in Later Life." *International Journal of Women's Studies* 8(2): 158-66.

Hansson, R. O., and J. H. Remondet. 1988. "Old Age and Widowhood: Issues of Personal Control and Independence." *Journal of Social Issues* 44(3): 159-74.

Harvey, C. D., and H. M. Bahr. 1974. "Widowhood, Morale, and Affiliation." *Journal of Marriage and the Family* 36: 97-106.

————. 1980. *The Sunshine Widows: Adapting to Sudden Bereavement.* Lexington, MA: Lexington Books.

Heikkinen, R.-L. 1996. "Experienced Aging as Elucidated by Narratives." Pp. 187-204 in *Aging and Biography: Explorations in Adult Development*, ed. J. E. Birren, G. M. Kenyon, J.-E. Ruth, J. J. R. Schoots and T. Svensson. New York: Springer.

Heinemann, G. 1982. "Why Study Widowed Women: A Rationale." *Women and Health* 7: 17-22.

Heinemann, G., and P. Evans. 1990. "Widowhood: Loss, Change and Adaptation." Pp. 142-67 in *Family Relationships in Later Life*, ed. T. Brubaker. Beverly Hills, CA: Sage.

Hochschild, A. R. 1973. *The Unexpected Community: Portrait of an Old-Age Subculture.* Englewood Cliffs, NJ: Prentice Hall.

————. 1979. "Emotion Work, Feeling Rules, and Social Structure." *American Journal of Sociology*, 85(3): 551-75.

————. 1989. *The Second Shift: Working Parents and the Revolution at Home.* New York: Viking.

————. 1997. *The Time Bind: When Work Becomes Home and Home Becomes work.* New York: Metropolitan Books.

Keith, J., C. L. Fry, A. P. Glascock, C. Ikels, J. Dickerson-Putman, H. C. Harpending and P. Draper. 1994. *The Aging Experience: Diversity and Commonality across Cultures.* Thousand Oaks, CA: Sage.

Kübler-Ross, E. 1969. *On Death and Dying.* New York: Macmillan.

Lindemann, E. 1944. "Symptomatology and Management of Acute Grief." *American Journal of Psychiatry* 101: 141-48.

Lopata, H. Z. 1973 *Widowhood in an American City.* Cambridge, MA: Schenkman.

————. 1975. "Couple-Companionate Relationships in Marriage and Widowhood." Pp. 119-49 in *Old Family/New Family: Interpersonal Relationships*, ed. N. Glazer-Malbin. New York: D. Van Nostrand.

————. 1976. "Widows as a Minority Group." Pp. 348-55 in *Contemporary Social Gerontology*, ed. B. D. Bell. Springfield, IL: Charles C. Thomas.

————. 1979. *Women as Widows: Support Systems.* New York: Elsevier.

————. 1981. "Widowhood and Husband Sanctification." *Journal of Marriage and the Family* 43: 439-50.

_____. 1988. "Support Systems of American Urban Widowhood." *Journal of Social Issues* 44(3): 113-28.

Lopata, H. Z. 1996. *Current Widowhood: Myths and Realities*. Thousand Oaks, CA: Sage.

Lund, D. A., D. A. Redburn, M. S. Juretich and M. S. Caserta. 1989. "Resolving Problems Implementing Bereavement Self-Help Groups." Pp. 203-16 in *Older Bereaved Spouses: Research with Practical Applications*, ed. D. A. Lund. New York: Hemisphere.

MacRae, H. 1990. "Older Women and Identity Maintenance in Later Life." *Canadian Journal on Aging* 9(3): 248-67.

_____. 1995. "Stigma Management: The Case of Alzheimer Disease." A paper presented at the 13th Annual Conference of The Atlantic Association of Sociology and Anthropology, 12-15 October, University of New Brunswick/St. Thomas University, Fredericton, NB.

_____. 1996. "Strong and Enduring Ties: Older Women and Their Friends." *Canadian Journal on Aging* 15(3): 374-92.

Mancini, J. A., and R. Blieszner. 1989. "Aging Parents and Adult Children: Research Themes in Intergenerational Relations." *Journal of Marriage and the Family* 51 (May): 275-90.

March, K. 1995. "Perception of Adoption as Social Stigma: Motivation for Search and Reunion." *Journal of Marriage and the Family* 57 (August): 653-60.

Martin Matthews, A. 1991. *Widowhood in Later Life*. Toronto: Butterworths.

Matthews, S. H. 1979. *The Social World of Old Women: Management of Self-Identity*. Newbury Park, CA: Sage.

_____. 1986. *Friendships through the Life Course: Oral Biographies in Old Age*. Beverly Hills, CA: Sage.

McCall, G., and J. L. Simmons. 1966. *Identities and Interactions*. New York: Viking Press.

McCrae, R. R., and Costa, P. T. 1988. "Psychological Resilience among Widowed Men and Women: A 10-Year Follow-up of a National Sample." *Journal of Social Issues* 44: 129-42.

Mills, C. W. 1959. *The Sociological Imagination*. New York: Oxford University Press.

Morgan, L. A. 1984. "Changes in Family Interaction Following Widowhood." *Journal of Marriage and the Family* 46: 323-33.

_____. 1986. "The Financial Experience of Widowed Women: Evidence from the LRHS." *The Gerontologist* 26(6): 663-68.

Motenko, A. K. 1988. "Respite Care and Pride in Caregiving: The Experience of Six Older Men Caring for Their Disabled Wives." Pp. 104-27 in *Qualitative Gerontology*, ed. S. Reinharz and G. D. Rowles. New York: Springer.

National Council on Welfare. 1990. *Women and Poverty Revisited*. Ottawa: Minister of Supply and Services.

————. 1994. *Poverty Profile 1992*. Ottawa: Minister of Supply and Services.

————. 1996. *A Pension Primer*. Ottawa: Minister of Supply and Services.

Novak, M. 1997. *Aging and Society: A Canadian Perspective*. Toronto: ITP Nelson.

Oakley, A. 1981. "Interviewing Women: A Contradiction in Terms." Pp. 30-61 in *Doing Feminist Research*, ed. H. Roberts. London: Routledge.

O'Bryant, S. L., and R. O. Hansson. 1995. "Widowhood." Pp. 440-58 in *Handbook of Aging and the Family*, ed. R. Blieszner and V. H. Bedford. Westport, CT: Greenwood Press.

O'Bryant, S. L., and L. B. Straw. 1991. "Relationship of Previous Divorce and Previous Widowhood to Older Women's Adjustment to Recent Widowhood." *The Journal of Divorce and Remarriage* 15(3/4): 49-67.

Parkes, C. M. 1972. *Bereavement: Studies in Grief in Adult Life*. New York: International Universities Press.

————. 1975. "Determinants of Outcome Following Bereavement." *Omega* 6: 303-23.

————. 1988. "Bereavement as a Psychosocial Transition: Processes of Adaptation to Change." *Journal of Social Issues* 44(3): 53-65.

Prosterman, A. 1996. "Community and Societal Responses to American Widows." Pp. 88-209 in *Current Widowhood: Myths and Realities*, H. Z. Lopata. Thousand Oaks, CA: Sage.

Reinharz, S. 1993. *On Becoming a Social Scientist*. 4th ed. New Brunswick, NJ: Transaction.

Rook, K. S. 1989. "Strains in Older Adult friendship." Pp. 166-94 in *Older Adult Friendship: Structure and Process*, ed. R. G. Adams and R. Blieszner. Newbury Park, CA: Sage.

Rosenmayr, L. 1977. "The Family—A Source of Hope for the Elderly?" Pp. 132-57 in *Family, Bureaucracy, and the Elderly*, ed. E. Shanas and M. B. Sussman. Durham, NC: Duke University Press.

Rosenthal, C. J., and P. Dawson. 1991. "Wives of Institutionalized Elderly Men: The First Stage of the Transition to Quasi-Widowhood." *Journal of Aging and Health* 3(3): 315-34.

Silverman, P. R. 1986. *Widow to Widow*. New York: Springer.

Simmel, G. 1971 [1908]. "The Stranger." Pp. 143-50 in *On Individuality and Social Forms*, ed. D. Levine. Chicago: Chicago University Press.

Smith, L. L. 1991. "Journeying through Widowhood: The Crystallization of a New Reality." Ph.D. dissertation, University of California at San Francisco.

Suttles, G. D. 1970. "Friendship as a Social Institution." Pp. 95-135 in *Social Relationships*, ed. G. C. McCall. Chicago: Aldine.

*The New Brunswick Extra-Mural Hospital: A Response to the Future.* N.d.

Thompson, L. W., D. Gallagher-Thompson, A. Futterman, M. J. Gilewski and J. Peterson. 1991. "The Effects of Late-Life Spousal Bereavement Over a 30-Month Interval." *Psychology and Aging* 6: 434-41.

Townsend, P. 1957. *The Family Life of Old People: An Inquiry in East London*. London: Routledge & Kegan Paul.

Unruh, D. R. 1983. *Invisible Lives: Social Worlds of the Aged*. Beverley Hills, CA: Sage.

Vachon, M. L. S., and S. K. Stylianos. 1988. The Role of Social Support in Bereavement. *Journal of Social Issues* 44(3): 175-90.

Vachon, M. L. S., J. Rogers, W. A. Lyall, W. J. Lancee, A. R. Sheldon and S. J. J. Freeman. 1982. "Predictors and Correlates of Adaptation to Conjugal Bereavement." *American Journal of Psychiatry* 139(8): 998-1002.

van den Hoonaard, D. K. 1992. "The Aging of a Florida Retirement Community." Unpublished Ph.D. dissertation, Loyola University of Chicago.

_____. 1994. "Paradise Lost: Widowhood in a Florida Retirement Community." *Journal of Aging Studies* 8(2): 121-32.

_____. 1995. "The First Question: The Construction of Widowhood through Narrative Interviewing." Paper presented to the Qualitative Analysis Conference, McMaster University, Hamilton, ON.

_____. 1997. "Identity Foreclosure: Women's Experiences of Widowhood as Expressed in Autobiographical Accounts." *Ageing and Society* 17: 533-51.

van den Hoonaard, W. C. 1997. *Working with Sensitizing Concepts: Analytical Field Research*. Thousand Oaks, CA: Sage.

Weber, M. 1949. *The Methodology of the Social Sciences*, Trans. E. A. Shils and H. A. Finch. Glencoe, IL: Free Press.

Wortman, C. B., and R. C. Silver. 1990. "Successful Mastery of Bereavement and Widowhood: A Life-Course Perspective." Pp. 225-64 in *Successful Aging: Perspectives from the Behavioral Sciences*, ed. P. B. Baltes and M. M. Baltes. New York: Cambridge University Press.

Wright, P. H. 1991. "Gender Differences in Adults' Same- and Cross-Gender Friendships." Pp. 197-221 in *Older Adult Friendship: Structure and Process*, ed. R. G. Adams and R. Blieszner. Newbury Park, CA: Sage.

Wu, Z. 1995. "Remarriage after Widowhood: A Marital History Study of Older Canadians." *Canadian Journal on Aging* 14(4): 719-36.

# Index